By Chelsea Handler

I'll Have What She's Having

I'll Have What She's Having

Chelsea Handler

THE DIAL PRESS
NEW YORK

Published in the United States by The Dial Press, an imprint of Random House, a division of Penguin Random House LLC, New York.

THE DIAL PRESS is a registered trademark and the colophon is a trademark of Penguin Random House LLC.

Hardback ISBN 978-0-593-59657-9
Ebook ISBN 978-0-593-59658-6

Printed in the United States of America on acid-free paper

randomhousebooks.com

9 8 7 6 5 4 3 2 1

FIRST EDITION

Book design by Ralph Fowler

This book is dedicated to flight attendants everywhere. You don't get enough credit for all the hard work you do, the travelers you endure, and the service you provide. As someone who spends a third of her life on planes, I would like to thank you for your patience, your service, and your pleasantness. Much of this book was written on planes, and I have seen firsthand how outrageous people can be. I've seen bare feet on planes, I've seen someone drying their underwear on a plane, and I've seen a passenger bring oysters on board, only to discard the shells they came with in a plastic bag for you to get rid of. I have seen you deal with people who refuse to wear masks, people who are inebriated, and people who mistreat you. You don't deserve any of that. You are heroes who deserve our utmost respect and kindness. Thank you for your service. I will always have your back on any plane with any asshole. If you see me on your flight and you are dealing with one of these assholes, please don't hesitate to come and get me. It would be my absolute pleasure to assist. We all need to respect our flight attendants. They are our sisters in the sky. And yes, I know there are male flight attendants, but most of them are sisters, too. With much love, I salute you.

To have and not to give is often worse than to steal.

—Marie von Ebner-Eschenbach

Contents

I'll Have What She's Having

Little Girl

When I was a little girl, I spent large parts of my day dreaming about the kind of woman I'd one day be. I wanted to fast-forward through all of my youth and misery, and become the more glamorous, successful, adult version of myself.

She would be nothing less than fierce, this woman I'd become. She would never have to worry about fitting in—she wouldn't be the type of person who valued herself based on other people's opinions. She wasn't going to be someone who followed what others did; she would be a leader. She'd be someone who would never have to rely on another person for anything.

She would be confident and never hesitate to stick her neck out for other people. Anyone who needed a hand would be able to depend on her. She'd be strong and she'd be beautiful, with a mind so sharp no one could ever call her just a pretty face. She'd be so much more than that.

She'd be able to light up a room, and her light would spread, making others feel brighter, better. She would be passionate and fiery, and courageous. She'd never be afraid to tell the truth, no matter the consequences.

She'll be different, this woman. She'll set an example for all other women. She'll soar through the world, traveling the globe, leaving her mark everywhere she went.

She'll break some hearts and heal others. She'll have men at her feet, begging to be with her, and women at her feet, begging to be her friend. She'll cast a wide net, and have friends all around the world. She'll have different loves throughout her life—and then, maybe one true soul mate, an everlasting love. Or maybe not. She'll be a beautiful hurricane.

She'll be respected for many reasons. She'll love people passionately and save people's lives with her generosity. She'll be educated about global politics, read every book she can get her hands on, and speak multiple languages. She'll have certainty in her own opinion and the power to change others'. She'll have the courage of her own convictions and the boldness to know she is capable of whatever lies at the heart of her dreams. She will be the *baddest*. The best kind of bad. A matriarch.

This woman I'll become, she will never be silent.

She'll be brave, and strong, and able to get out of any bad situation. She will have the kind of bravery it takes to walk into a situation knowing that the worst could happen, and she'll jump in anyway. The type of bravery it takes to walk away from something or someone you love, knowing that you are walking away not in weakness but in strength. Knowing that you will survive, because you are a survivor. She'll be a survivor.

Why do I have to wait so long to get to be this woman? I'd wonder. *Childhood has been such a waste of my time.*

When we are children, the essence
of who we are is front and center.
We are unscathed by what can very often
be an ugly world. Bringing that child
into adulthood, even only for moments at a
time, is how we remain true to ourselves.
Hold on to that child tightly, as if she
were your own, because she is.

Hard Lemonade

A t ten years old, I decided to start my own lemonade business. I asked my sister Shana if she would be interested in going into business with me. She was five years my senior, and she insisted that in order for her to come on board, this would need to be a joint venture—we'd have to split everything fifty-fifty. I begrudgingly agreed, but I was firm in letting her know that I would be the one making most of the business decisions, and that in order to make some real money, we would be reimagining the lemonade stand business. Ours would be a *hard* lemonade stand, serving gin, whiskey, and tequila.

On our first day, we made thirteen dollars, and after splitting it down the middle, I was left with six dollars and fifty cents. This was not going to work. I needed a greater profit margin and less overhead. The bottom line was that I would have to find cheaper labor.

"You're fired," I told Shana as we walked down the dirt road back to our house with all of our lemonade equipment.

She tried to explain to me that I wasn't in a position to fire her, but I reminded her that it was my idea in the first place, and that she was welcome to start her own lemonade stand and become my competitor.

The next day, I went door-to-door in our neighborhood looking for staff. I knocked on each door, announced that I was Chelsea Handler, a ten-year-old business owner who was interested in hiring another child to work with, and if the employee insisted, I would allot a half hour of playtime after each shift. I was well aware that most children my age did not have the same work ethic I did.

That's when I met Nelson, another ten-year-old who seemed eager for a playmate. I started grooming Nelson right away. I took him back to my house and demonstrated the right ratio of lemonade to alcohol. I explained that our target market was the parents, and that our ancillary market would be their children—and that we would be giving straight lemonade to anyone who looked younger than Nelson.

On our first day in business together, Nelson and I made thirty-three dollars. When I handed him his commission, he couldn't believe his good fortune in meeting me.

"Stick with me, Nelson. I'll show you the way," I told him, tousling his hair, and dropping him off at his house.

By the end of our first week together, word had spread about our little lemonade bar, and business was booming. I made over $359 in that first week, and when I gave Nelson his commission of $3.59, he lost his marbles.

"This is more money than I would have made if I lost five teeth in the same week!" he exclaimed.

I didn't have the heart to explain that the tooth fairy, Santa Claus, and the Easter Bunny were not real. *This kid has a great work ethic,* I thought. *He's enthusiastic about bartending. Better to keep him motivated and delusional if I want to earn a serious living.*

First Class

My mother took me on my very first airplane ride across the country to visit my aunt and grandparents in Los Angeles when I was ten. There were four of us traveling, including my mother, and when we boarded the plane and walked past the first-class section, I stopped and sniffed around.

"This seems like my group," I told my mother. Instead, she ushered me down the aisle toward the very long coach section and whispered that the section I was referring to was "first class" and that we would never be flying first-class because there were five kids in our family and we couldn't afford it. *Speak for yourself,* I thought.

Once we got back from California, I was more motivated than ever to start earning some of my own cash. The writing was on the wall: if my family was content flying coach for the rest of their lives, we simply weren't on the same page, and I would, at some point, have to split ties with them.

My parents had a house on Martha's Vineyard where we'd spend the summer months. That year, when we arrived, I called every hotel in Edgartown and gave them my name and number in case any of their guests needed a babysitter. I was ten at the time, but I looked like I was fifteen, so I lied and said I was fifteen. I ended up spending that summer babysitting for a fourteen-year-old boy. His name was Jeremy and he had behavioral issues, which required me to regularly put him in time-outs. I babysat for Jeremy for the next three summers until he was seventeen and I was thirteen.

Thanks to my lemonade stand business and burgeoning babysitting empire, I had already saved thousands of dollars by the time I was twelve. So, when my mom announced that we would be flying to California for my grandfather's funeral, I walked down the street to my friend's house. Her mother was a travel agent, and I gave her three thousand dollars to purchase a first-class ticket to Los Angeles—for myself.

When we boarded the plane, I was with my two brothers and my mom. I located the seat identified on my ticket, stuffed my Barbie backpack into the overhead bin, sat down in my assigned seat, 2C, and looked at my family.

"I'll see you idiots at the end of the flight," I said.

I looked around at the passengers in first class, many of whom were drinking champagne. *These are my people,* I thought. *This is my group. This is where the woman I will become is going to sit.*

Cross-Country
Chicanery

At nineteen, I decided it was time to move to Los Angeles and become a celebrity. I didn't know what exact vocation I would end up in, but I had strong opinions about a lot of things, and I thought the world would be a better place if I shared them.

I had completed one and a half semesters at a community college in Morristown, New Jersey, where I realized rather quickly that I'd be better off skipping college and moving to California. I was very inspired by *Three's Company* and their lifestyle on that show. I was eager to strap on a pair of Rollerblades and stroll down the strand telling everyone, "Come and knock on *my* door."

When I told my parents my plan, they said they thought it was a good idea. In my father's words: "Good. Please go. I'll get one of the cars ready."

Being that he was a used-car dealer, he always had cars, but none of them were ever ready to actually drive. He hooked me up with an oil change and transmission check, and then bought me four new tires for my 1985 stick shift silver Audi Quattro. I had never seen my father as enthusiastic about spending money as he was about paying for those new tires. That's how happy he was that I was moving three thousand miles away. I dug that car, until I drove its transmission straight into the ground.

The night before I was set to drive across the country alone, my brother Glen came over to the house and told me he had met a bartender who also happened to be heading across country and was looking for a ride. My brothers have never been overly protective of me, and this was a classic example of how little regard for my safety they had.

"Sounds good. As long as he can afford to chip in for hotels and gas money," I told Glen.

The next night, I picked up a twenty-five- or twenty-six-year-old short blond man from his parents' house somewhere in northern New Jersey. I can't remember this person's name, but one of the first sentences out of his mouth was, "Should we drive to Harlem first and get some cocaine for the ride?"

I had experimented with cocaine before, but it wasn't a passion of mine at the time. I had zero to little interest in doing it while driving across country. But I was excited to go to Harlem with someone who knew their way around. Harlem had been off-limits when I was a teenager, and when we went to the city in high school, it was mostly to a nightclub called the Limelight, where we dropped acid and ecstasy. Cocaine seemed like an older person's drug, but I liked this guy's spunk, so we headed off to Harlem.

I sat in my car on 146th Street while he went inside a house for about twenty minutes and came out with a bag of cocaine the size of an airplane pillow. I had only seen bags of drugs that massive in the movies, and I was flabbergasted at the sheer volume. He reported that this was a pound of cocaine, and that it would be his contribution to the trip.

I told him that I didn't really do cocaine and that he would have to pitch in financially for lodging and gas, which I thought my brother had explained.

He clarified that it wasn't a problem, and that if I wanted the cash instead of the cocaine, we could easily sell some of it along the way. I envisioned myself driving across country while slowly transitioning into a coke dealer and then having to call my brother from behind bars upon my first arrest, probably in Texas.

From Harlem, we drove down to Maryland and headed for Route 66, which takes you straight across the country to California. There was a long detour through Washington, D.C., and many lanes were shut down on the highway for repair. By this time, it was late at night, and my passenger, whom I'll refer to as Dipsy Doodle, had taken out several large maps while also scooping cocaine out of the bag with his bank card and snorting it. I was confused by the panoply of maps. This was before cell phones and satellite navigation and all of that, but how many maps of one country did a person need? There are three highways that take you across the United States, and it is a pretty straight shot, so this behavior was suspect. All I could think of was my brother Glen and his lackluster ability to make choices that were in my best interest.

Dipsy Doodle was talking a lot about all the different options we had to zigzag across the country and all the national parks we could hit up on our way. I didn't have the patience to explain that we weren't going to "hit up" any national parks—that I was trying to get to my aunt's house in Bel Air as soon as humanly possible, and that the only reason he was with me was so I wouldn't have to drive across the country as a single nineteen-year-old female. Seeing the condition he was in made it clear that if anyone would be taking care of anyone in this situation, it would be me taking care of him and not the other way around.

By the time we got to Maryland, Dipsy Doodle hadn't stopped talking for four straight hours. I needed a break. I told him that we were going to have to pull over for the night at whatever Howard Johnson or Holiday Inn we found next. We checked into a room with two double beds, where Dipsy Doodle proceeded to lay out his map collection all over the coffee table and bed, continuing to talk about all the sightseeing we could do.

He was somehow under the impression that we were on a retirement trip of sorts and that we had all the time in the world to explore every nook and cranny of America. At this point, I was lying in my bed, calculating how fast we could actually get to Los Angeles if we only stopped for gas. Dipsy Doodle hadn't even bothered to bring his suitcase into the hotel because, he explained, he'd be up all night doing cocaine—and mapping out our drive.

I fell asleep to the sound of him snorting cocaine off one of the maps, and when I woke up in the morning, he was pacing back and forth throughout the room, looking like Dog the Bounty Hunter. I don't know if Dog the Bounty Hunter does copious amounts of cocaine, but he sure looks like he does.

I got up, brushed my teeth, might have taken a shower, and then told my driving partner that I was going to pack up the car and that I'd be right back. When I got to the parking lot where my car was, I opened the trunk, took his suitcase out, placed it in the parking space next to my car, and drove away. You didn't have to be a member of Mensa to realize this guy was going to be a massive liability.

I hauled ass across country avoiding all truck stops and only stopped for gas until I got pulled over in Amarillo, Texas, on Route 66 by a state trooper. State troopers seemed petrifying to me at nineteen years old, and I was definitely scared. The trooper strode up to my driver's side window with a large black German shepherd, who proceeded to go apeshit when he got to the trunk area of my car—which was where Dipsy Doodle had stored the cocaine for an hour before we got to Maryland when he became paranoid the cops were following us.

The state trooper asked me to step out of my car after I handed him my license and registration, and then sternly directed me to take fifty steps behind the car. I stood on the side of Route 66 with eighteen-wheelers passing me, imagining a life behind bars all before I even had the chance to make a name for myself in Hollywood. I devised my defense if the trooper and his very intimidating wide-brimmed trooper's hat put me in handcuffs: I would insist that they dust my car for fingerprints in order to prove there had been another person in my car whom I had the good sense to leave in Maryland, and that they could test me for cocaine and realize I had nothing to do with the drug. My story would be that once I knew that Dipsy Doodle had cocaine on him, I kicked him out of the car. The fact that I drove him in my car to pick up the cocaine would be omitted from the tale. As another eighteen-wheeler blew past me standing on the side of the highway, I almost fell over at the intensity of the wind.

After twenty minutes of a thorough examination of my car, the trooper informed me that I was free to go because they had not found anything incriminating, even though the dog's reaction suggested otherwise.

I pulled back onto the highway with both legs shaking and didn't stop for anything other than gas for the rest of the trip. I arrived in California seventeen hours later. When I reached my aunt and uncle's house in Los Angeles, I told them the whole story. My uncle responded by asking me to confirm that all the cocaine was indeed gone. "I haven't done cocaine in ages," he said. "I wouldn't mind a big fat line."

That night, I called my brother Glen, who was now on Martha's Vineyard with my parents. I thanked him for setting me up with a complete basket case to drive across the country with and told him that his judgment needed an update.

In very Glen-like fashion, he seemed nonplussed. "Yes," he said, "I heard your driving companion had to hire a taxi from Maryland back to Morris Plains, New Jersey."

"Good for him," I said. "Our first order of business was going to Harlem so 'your friend' could buy a pound of cocaine."

I went on to tell Glen about being pulled over in the panhandle of Texas, and that if I hadn't left my driving "companion" in Maryland,

I'd be in a Texas state prison right now getting finger blasted by a female prison guard.

"So, thanks for that referral," I said, and hung up.

No one was going to stop me from getting to L.A. and starting my life. When an obstacle arose in the form of Dipsy Doodle, I removed said obstacle.

Temporary Employment

The best way to describe my early years in Los Angeles would be to say: I scraped by. I was either getting paid by focus groups, which meant sitting in a room with twenty strangers who were also getting paid thirty dollars an hour to give our opinion on new products, or working with a temporary employment agency, which required me to pretend to be a secretary in various professional settings. This is not where any talent of mine lies. I couldn't even transfer calls from the main desk to different offices without getting screamed at.

I was never invited back to any job twice, and at one law firm one of the partners called the front desk to ask me who the "blond bimbo" temping was, and when the hell were we going to get rid of her.

"Uhhh . . . ," I stammered. "I think you're talking to her. I can just leave," I said, putting the phone down, grabbing my things, and hauling ass out the door. The timing couldn't have been more perfect, because I had been fantasizing about a chocolate Frappuccino all morning, and there was a Starbucks on the bottom floor of the building.

I didn't care that he called me stupid. I knew I wasn't stupid.

I have been called stupid many times in my life. I have been called dumb, obnoxious, trashy, raunchy, crass, a fake, and various other things throughout my career. I have been all of those things at certain moments, but not one of those words encapsulates who I am. None of the things other people have called me has ever really mattered. What other people say about you only matters if you believe what they are saying is true.

I knew that I didn't have the type of brain to work in an office, or with any sort of technology—and this was before the advent of present-day technology and what we are dealing with today. When it comes to technology, having my hands tied behind my back and my head stuffed inside a watermelon would yield the same results as having full use of my eyes, ears, and fingers. At any moment, I am one JPEG away from stabbing myself in the vagina.

Even in my early twenties, when I was broke, bouncing from one job to another, borrowing money from anyone I could, I knew I had value. I knew that if I kept chugging away, I would find the people who would recognize that value. I wasn't going to let some guy who worked in an office building, and would for the rest of his life, make me feel bad about not being able to transfer a phone call—just because he had a law degree.

The inability to transfer a phone call only further cemented my suspicion that I wouldn't be good at anything that required me to sit inside an office. I took getting yelled at that day as a sign that I was headed in the right direction, that I needed to use my voice, and that temporary office work was one more thing I tried and could now cross off my list.

This day lives in my memory, because if this had happened on a different day a week earlier, or a week later, I would have had a different reaction. I would have felt shame at being called stupid, inadequate for not being able to transfer a phone call, and I would have allowed a stranger to make me feel terrible about myself. If this had happened on a different day, I would have walked out of that law office in tears.

None of that happened, because he caught me on a day when I felt good about myself, hopeful about the future—even though my life was anything but stable in that moment. I was my true self that day, and I was grounded in the idea that I would set out to do what I came out to California to do: to make a living at being me.

In the grand scheme of things, this man didn't matter at all. He serves as a reminder to me on the days when I do not feel strong, confident, or hopeful to tap into the version of me who does. To know that every feeling passes, and that no moment in time is permanent, and that the truest version of who we all are is confident, hopeful, and resilient.

Montreal Comedy Bomb

After about five years of doing stand-up pretty regularly around Los Angeles and opening for other comics on the road, I was offered my very first spot at the Just for Laughs Montreal Comedy Festival.

This festival was the industry standard for an up-and-coming comic, signaling that you were on your way to big things. It also meant you would be seen by everyone in the industry who could hire you.

Once I arrived in Montreal, it became clear through my manager at the time that there was a buzz about me and my showcase. Everyone would be there. It would be standing room only, and every person in the audience would be someone who could make a decision about putting me on television. I felt like everything I had come to Los Angeles for was about to come together, and that I finally would be recognized for my value in the industry I wanted to blaze through.

I was prepared because I had been practicing this ten-minute set for months, and I knew this was going to be a very important night.

I bombed badly. Very badly. It was mortifying. I got onstage, my timing was off, my jokes fell flat, and it all fell apart at the seams. Upon realizing how quiet the room had become, I sped through the rest of my set and scurried offstage. I was too embarrassed to hang around afterward, and I was too humiliated to see the pity on the faces of all the people who had just watched me tank. My manager didn't know what to say, because it was an embarrassment for him as well. He had spent the last two weeks inviting every industry person he knew to the show.

Zach Galifianakis walked me to my hotel room that night. When we got to my room, he told me, "You're going to want to be alone for a while." This was at a time in my twenties when I needed other people to make me feel better when I was feeling bad. But there was no one who could do that. He was right. There was no one to call, and no one who was going to make me feel better.

That night was one of the worst nights of my early adulthood. I sat in my room, wondering what the hell I was going to do with my life. I had never felt so ashamed. How could I have blown such a big opportunity? How long would it take me to redeem myself? And how would that even happen? I didn't call anyone from my family, which I always did after a successful show. I sat alone, in shock, and cried, like my life was ending—before it had even begun.

I had another show the next night, which went a lot better, but it didn't matter, because no one from the industry came. My manager tried to round up some executives to come give me another shot, but everyone had moved on to the next talent who had buzz around them. No one was interested in offering me a second chance, and I really couldn't blame them. The idea that so many people thought I was untalented made me physically ill. It was the first big professional failure of my career, and it hurt badly.

When I got back to Los Angeles that Monday, my manager called and told me that Grace Wu from NBC hadn't been able to make the show in Montreal, and was asking if I had any sets that week that she could see. Grace was the only top-level executive who hadn't been at my show in Montreal, and she wanted to see me perform.

I called my friend Sam Brown and booked myself on a show for the very next night at a club called Luna Park.

I crushed that show at Luna Park. I did the same exact set, and because I had nothing to lose, I was calm, secure, and my timing was on. The pressure was off, and I went up there and did my thing, and I did exactly what I had hoped to do at the festival three nights earlier.

The next day, I got a call from my manager, who told me NBC was making me an offer for a development deal for my own TV show and I would be paid a hundred thousand dollars.

When people say, "Everything happens for a reason," I always think, *What reason?* Perhaps I needed a dose of humility. Perhaps it was a lesson in counting your chickens before they hatch. Who knows. What I do know is that at twenty-five years old, I had one of the worst sets and career lows of my life, and within seventy-two hours everything had completely turned around. Suddenly I was able to stop waitressing, and start meeting with writers about my very own TV show. It took only seventy-two hours for every feeling I had in Montreal to be turned on its head, and for the future to be bright again. I think of this moment often when things aren't going well, or when a friend of mine is going through a tough time. So often, we are ready to give up or throw in the towel when, right around the corner, there is a pocket of sunshine we hadn't known was headed straight for us. Even in my lowest moments, I keep my head geared toward the sky, because I'm no longer in the business of missing rainbows.

Everything can change in an instant. And more important, it doesn't matter how many people say no. All you need is one person to say yes.

Jane Fonda

got an email from Jane Fonda one day that said, "Hi, Chelsea, It's Jane. I was wondering if you could come over to my house for dinner. I'd like to talk to you about a couple of things."

This sounded ominous. I had been friends with Jane for at least ten years and it seemed like sort of a terse email to get from her, but since Jane Fonda is a fucking legend, I didn't hesitate to respond with "Of course. Let me know when."

"Tonight at seven."

Jesus, I thought. *This sounds like I'm in trouble*—and I was exactly right. I was in trouble.

When I got to Jane's house, her chef opened the door, walked me inside, and asked if I wanted something to drink. "No, thank you," I answered, thinking, *If I'm about to be reprimanded, I want to be fully alert for my defense.*

Jane's demeanor seemed a bit cold, and I was anxious to find out exactly what I had done. As we sat for dinner and I was offered another drink that I declined, Jane asked me if I knew why she had asked me over for dinner.

"No," I replied.

"You may have noticed I was a little icy toward you when I saw you at Shonda Rhimes's fundraiser for Congressman John Lewis."

The event she was talking about had been three months prior, and the truth was, I had noticed she was a little icy toward me. But I hadn't obsessed over it, because at that point, I was bouncing through life with no direction or intention and other people's feelings were not my problem. If I got a negative vibe from someone, I never overanalyzed it, because I wasn't grounded, and I didn't overthink anything. When I am grounded, I am as solid as a tree. When I'm not, I'm more like a leaf. I can say that now, because I know what the difference is.

"You behaved badly at my party. From the moment you came in, you had a black cloud hanging over you and you insulted people and it brought the whole party down. I don't know what drugs you were on, but a few people told me you were horrible to them. I don't get it," she said. "Why did you even come if you were in that kind of mood?"

Wow, I thought. *This is a* doublefucksywhoopsiedoodle. Jane Fonda calling me out on my badly behaved self was as serious as it gets.

This was definitely not the woman I had dreamed of becoming.

It was embarrassing, painful, and definitely cringeworthy, but I didn't let any of those things diminish the fact that Jane had taken the time out of her life to be honest with me. I needed someone to do that with me, and even in that moment of shame I knew she would never have to speak to me about my behavior again because that's what that kind of honesty deserves: action.

I had just started going to therapy, so there was comfort in knowing I could bring this back to my therapist and have him help me digest and correct my behavior. But on a bigger note, Jane's admonishment made me understand and think about what it is I am trying to put out into this world. Definitely not what I was doing at Jane's party. The truth of the matter was: Who knows what drugs I was on? It could have been anything. It's my state of mind that determines my behavior on drugs, and if I'm in a good place in my life, and I'm grounded, drugs are fun, and so am I; if I'm in a bad state of mind or in a bad time of my life, drugs will only make me defensive or angry, and that's when I bite.

What struck me in that moment was Jane's brutal honesty. Something that has defined my entire career, but something I had never been on the receiving side of. I promptly ordered a martini, we continued our dinner, and I told her that while this news was hard to hear, I had been in therapy for the past two months because I knew something was up with me, and that I had in fact been dealing with the issue at hand—my deep anger.

"Good," she told me. "Go find out what your problem is, because your gifts are plentiful, and sometimes people with the most gifts have the easiest time throwing them in the trash. Don't be a product of your environment, Chelsea. Make your environment be a product of you."

This was the definition of sisterhood.

Happiness is an attitude. I choose it.
Even when it doesn't choose me.
I'll chase it around all day long until it gathers
me back up in its good graces.

Now What?

wo months before my dinner with Jane Fonda, I was giving an early morning speech in front of a few hundred people at a women's event in Los Angeles, when my leg started to shake. I shifted my weight back and forth in an attempt to disguise what was happening, but then both of my legs started shaking, and then the shaking turned to trembling. My face got hot, and I felt moisture gathering in both armpits and at the back of my neck. I felt a panic set in that I hadn't experienced before. I looked to find a chair on the stage behind me and sat down for the rest of my speech. I had never had a panic attack before, and was loath to admit that was what was happening. As I was walking out of the event after my speech, the organizer came up to me and asked if everything was okay. I had no explanation for what had happened, and I was mortified.

"Yeah, I'm just getting sick," I told her, avoiding eye contact. "I had a slight fever this morning, but I didn't want to cancel," I lied, turning myself into a hero. I couldn't bear the thought of anyone thinking of me as anything less than the confident bulldozer I had become. I was not about to be associated with someone who was unsure of themselves. I made a living by literally standing up and speaking, and there was no way I was going to let this new anxiety send my career into a nosedive

A couple of months later, when I started my Netflix talk show, the leg shaking began happening each night when I would come out to do my monologue. After a few nights of this, I moved my monologue to the desk so that I could sit while reading it. I was terrified because something had shifted, and nothing about my Netflix show or how I was feeling seemed right.

Everything that had been working for me my whole life was suddenly not working for me anymore. I wasn't grounded, I wasn't confident, and I was second-guessing all of my decisions. I wasn't the person who I had been during my seven years on *Chelsea Lately,* or who I had been during any of my Netflix documentary series just a year earlier. Something was different and it was unsettling. It felt like I was floating around, unsure of where to land, or if I even had the landing capabilities necessary to refocus. That woman I had dreamed of becoming hadn't even been on my mind in recent years. I had lost sight of her and this great sense of unease had occupied my mind and had taken over. Something was bubbling up inside me, and when I tried to ignore it, the feeling only intensified. With my self-reliability threatened, I knew I had to get help. I hated the idea of therapy, but I hated this loss of confidence even more. I was hoping this would be a problem easily remedied over three or four one-hour sessions. Instead, I spent the next two years in psychotherapy twice a week.

At the end of my two-year stint with my therapist Dan, I felt like a break was in order. If someone told me I had to go to another two years of therapy or that I had to spend the next two years at Mar-a-Lago sharing a bed with Donald Trump . . . well, I would have chosen therapy, but you get my drift.

I was eager to start applying what I had learned in therapy to my everyday life, in a practical way, without Dan. I had become so wrapped up in myself, and all of this therapy and self-discovery were not helping me disentangle that. Ironically, the act of pursuing a less self-absorbed perspective very directly conflicts with having to talk about yourself for hours ad infinitum. It is one big loop-de-loop of a no-fun zone.

Therapy was exhausting in the sense that every new development or idea led to a period of intense self-awareness followed by waves of acute self-consciousness coupled with endless self-recrimination. This was an overcorrection on my part, and I needed to stop looking outward and thinking about what people thought of me, or feeling shame at how many people I had offended over the years. I needed to pivot toward thinking about the type of person I wanted to be, rather than obsessing on the history of my behavior.

Each day was a new discovery and a step closer to understanding awareness and energy and all the scientific things that aren't taken seriously enough by society, because they aren't easily measured. I was beginning to feel the benefits of meditation, and when I was giving off good vibes or when I was frustrated or depleted and giving off low vibes. Jane Fonda had gifted me with her honesty, and I wasn't going to let her down.

A teacher friend of mine once described the school year as one of learning and the summer as the time where you absorb what you learned. There are cycles of planting and cycles of harvesting. I liked this philosophy, and I applied it to therapy. There is a time for studying, followed by a time of absorption, followed by the time where you start applying all the new tools you've acquired to your life.

I was still in that post-therapy fog of being able to name all of my behaviors and shortcomings that had led me to be so closed off to love and judgmental, but I was also confused as to how to move forward with my newfound repository of information. I had to blend my fresh awareness with the good parts of my old personality while also dropping the behaviors and habits that were hurtful to me and to the people in my life.

I once had a friend come over because she was worried about her new haircut and she knew I would tell her the truth. When she arrived, I confirmed to her that it was indeed the worst she had ever looked. My friend spent that day at my house crying, and after three hours I lost my patience and reprimanded her for caring so much about her hair.

"It's going to grow back at some point," I scolded her. "You can't be one of these people who is so consumed with the way you look. It's fucking hair!" I said this to her as my eyes were swollen and covered in bruises from a CO_2 laser, which prevented me from going out in public for the following ten days.

I knew my judgment of others could be harsh, and that I was always eager to share my opinions, whether helpful or hurtful. My new outlook allowed me to see how unnecessary it was to share every thought or harsh criticism.

Therapy is a tricky endeavor. You can be interested in the subject, and believe it is working, only to find yourself completely losing your shit over not being able to work the Sonos in your house. It's a lot of two steps forward, and just when you think you have graduated, you're taking two very large steps back in the direction you thought you were leaving.

I kept auditioning new versions of myself to see which one seemed like the best direction to head in. After discussing with Dan ad nauseam the idea that it wasn't my responsibility to be the life of the party or the most entertaining person at a dinner, I entered into what became a confusing time of course correcting. I found myself at more than one dinner party where I barely said a word. I had stopped inserting myself into other people's problems, and I was learning the power of keeping my opinions to myself. My friends became confused and slightly alarmed.

"What's your story? You're not talking at all," my friend Jen asked me privately, during a party at another friend's house.

"It's not my responsibility to entertain everyone," I told her. "I need to listen instead of talk all the time."

"So . . . what? Now you have a different personality?" she asked.

"I don't know," I told her. "I don't know that you can change your personality. I'm trying to change my behavior."

"Okay," she said. "But you're pretty boring tonight. How long is this self-reflection going to take? I mean, you've been in therapy for two years. We want Chelsea back."

That was the problem. Some of my friends didn't want me to change at all, but I wasn't going to be the same old Chelsea. I wanted to grow and evolve into whatever the newer, better version of me was, while also taking the good parts of old Chelsea with me.

It became a burden to have to explain to everyone what I was learning about myself and how I was experimenting with different behaviors, so I just stopped socializing so much, and I started hanging out alone. *There was a woman I had to find.*

Woman Up

When I was wrapping up therapy, it was mutually agreed that we would end my Netflix talk show. It wasn't performing well, and I wasn't performing well, either.

I was relieved to have a break from working. My childhood reading turned into a lifelong habit, and I spent the next two months reading as many self-help books as I could get my hands on, and embedding myself in the art of getting to the other side. I read *Letting Go, The Untethered Soul, The Four Agreements, The Art of Living, The Art of Happiness, The Power of Now, Attached, 10% Happier.* I even read *What to Expect When You're Expecting,* thinking maybe I could fill in the blanks where my parents had come up short. I also read a few other parenting books in the hope that I could learn a thing or two about parenting my inner child. Most self-help books pretty much say the same thing, but certain ideas resonate. I listened to ten conversations between Eckhart Tolle and Oprah about the meaning of consciousness and how to loosen your grip on things that you can't control, understanding that you are not your thoughts but the awareness of your thoughts. I would listen to these episodes again, and again, until I started to understand what the hell they were talking about. I was beginning to recognize the difference between my shadow self and my real self, and the distinction between ego and consciousness.

What I really wanted was for Oprah to counsel me directly, but she had interviewed me years earlier, and I got the distinct impression she found me arrogant, as I most likely had been.

I was unsure of which direction I was headed in, if I was even in the right career, if anyone even valued me or my contributions, or worst of all, if anyone would even notice if I just disappeared.

I decided to chill out with any drugs and alcohol, thinking that having a clear head for this portion of learning would be optimal. It seemed smarter to look within, to spend this time working out, eating healthy, and getting my mind in the best possible shape. I treated this period of my life like I was getting a master's degree in psychology.

I wanted to know as much as possible, and I was also noticing that without pot, and by implementing twenty minutes of meditation each day, the ADD I had diagnosed myself with years prior seemed to be lifting. This was an unexpected development, because cannabis had originally been my gateway drug into meditation—but, as with most things in my life, I had overdone it. I had been mindlessly getting high daily, and I would lose my train of thought walking down the hallway. I'd get distracted and inevitably end up rifling through the refrigerator thirty to forty times a day in the hopes that all the ingredients inside would have somehow magically merged with each other to produce an entirely new dish.

Without the distraction of weed, mushrooms, and the news, I was able to harness my interest and stay focused for hours at a time without checking my phone. I was beginning to feel the shift and clarity of mind that serious therapy generates, along with the ability to finally sit still. I wanted to fill myself up in other ways, and I recognized in myself creative sparks and interests that had been dormant for years.

I started writing my last book, *Life Will Be the Death of Me,* about my experience in therapy because I wanted to share my learnings with anyone who had been through similar pain, anger, delayed grief, denial, or a lack of self-awareness. I wanted to help as many people as I could while also putting into words all the mind-bending information I had gleaned. When I asked my therapist Dan for his permission to use his name in my book, he said he wanted to think about it, because the doctor-patient confidentiality is an ethical construct that should not be broken by a doctor. I reminded him I was the one breaking that pact, and I also informed him that the book would most likely be a *New York Times* bestseller. Dan hadn't known I had even written any books, and when the book debuted at the No. 1 spot on the *New York Times* list, I felt like I had stepped back onto the track I had fallen off.

To promote the book, I went on a speaking tour around the country. I would have different celebrities, personalities, or authors interview me onstage. I know now that I set it up that way because I was scared. I hadn't done stand-up for six years, and I was afraid that I no longer had the talent—but I wasn't willing to admit that to myself until I was halfway through the book tour and I recognized what I was doing.

That's when I decided it was time to woman up and throw any insecurities out the window and return to my roots. So, I added another twenty dates where I would be alone onstage, taking the very serious material from my last book and weaving it with the funny parts, to make a one-woman show. At the tail end of the tour, I sold that show as a stand-up special to HBO Max and titled it *Evolution*. This felt like a triumph. All of this work I had done on myself brought me back to the very thing that had launched my career. Now here I was, starting anew. This was a big moment for me, a sign that I was headed in the right direction; that I was in a very real way coming home to myself.

This is who I am, I thought. *This is what I'm supposed to be doing. Sharing my truth with others. Being bold with my honesty, and living in a loud, brave way. Making sure people know they are not alone.*

The Beginning
of the Beginning

The timing of COVID couldn't have been better for me and my self-exploration. I had been given orders from my therapist to spend more time alone, something I had avoided my whole life, and then, suddenly, I was receiving orders from Dr. Fauci to do the same. *No problem,* I thought.

If COVID taught me anything, it was how much I enjoy the pleasure of my own company.

I'd get up, take some mushrooms, read about the history of Cuba, then polish that off with some David Sedaris, and then around happy hour I would make myself a feast of frozen plant-based chicken nuggets while enjoying the mandate of absolutely no socializing. No doctor or scientist had to tell me twice to stop hanging out with other people. Everyone had been annoying the shit out of me for my entire life, and with the help of therapy I had finally come to understand the importance of being able to spend some quality time by myself.

Nothing serves as a better reminder to not having children than setting your alarm for 10:00 a.m. on a Monday to remind yourself to take mushrooms. If you've ever taken mushrooms, walked outside into your backyard, and talked to what you thought was a tree for two hours before realizing you were talking to your landscaper, you're probably single, too. Have you ever taken mushrooms *with* your landscaper? Do you know who has time for these kinds of life experiences? People who don't have children.

My sister Simone called me three weeks into lockdown.

"The kids and I are on top of each other, and everyone is starting to lose it. We're thinking of driving down to Los Angeles with the dogs and moving into your house so we can have more room to 'spread out.'"

The "kids" my sister was referring to were her three adult children, ages twenty-four, twenty-one, and eighteen. The two dogs were my sister's dog Boston—who had been passed around our family like a used car—and my nephew Jakey's Australian shepherd, Tucker, who remains the most annoying dog I've ever encountered. When Tucker's around, you can't leave doggy bowls out, because he doesn't understand how to drink out of a bowl without turning the kitchen into a water park. He is high energy, wants to be thrown a ball close to 150 times a day, and is definitely not my *type*.

On April 1, 2020, my house was invaded. It didn't take very long after my family moved in for me to see the difference between males and females in terms of how they take up space. I of course have witnessed this before, but I assumed the younger men in my family, and also the younger generation, would have become a little more self-aware after everything our society has learned in the past five years about the imbalance of power between men and women. With all the available information out there, I was naive enough to think that centuries of misogyny and entitlement would somehow diminish in the span of a few cultural and political movements. I was wrong. Apparently, evolution takes a long time, intergenerational habits will take eons to turn around, and the planet will most likely explode before that happens. Instead of a major reconciliation between the sexes, *Roe v. Wade* was overturned, which seemed very clearly to be a repercussion of the #MeToo movement. If women were going to start telling on men, then we would need a very strong reminder by men of who was really in charge.

During COVID, I watched as my two nieces were very conscientious of each other and of everyone else in the house. They wore AirPods for their work or school Zooms, and the two of them would get dressed respectably each day, in full outfits—with footwear. My sister has an extremely annoying job in the health-care field that required her to be on Zooms from 9:00 to 5:00 daily. (She also wore AirPods.) My nephew, on the other hand, is a sports journalist who spends his days watching replays, and for some reason he seemed to believe the consideration of wearing AirPods didn't apply to him.

One of my biggest takeaways from my work with Dan Siegel was learning about nonreactive behavior: How to take something in, consider it, and then formulate a response instead of reacting to everything in the moment and with a temper. To understand that most things are not in your control, and that one of the only things that you can control is your reaction. You can choose to take something in, and to be calm and thoughtful with your response—or you can blow your gasket every time you hear or see something you don't like, like I did for my entire childhood and early adulthood.

When I walked downstairs one morning to find my nephew Jakey wearing mesh basketball shorts and lounging on the sofa in my living room with one knee propped under his chin and the other leg strewn across the cushions, I noticed there was a large tear in his shorts, which essentially split his balls in two. No amount of therapy could contain my outrage.

"I'm sorry," I said, leaning in. "Can I get you a *cigar*?" I asked, reacting to my field of vision being violated. "Close your legs, Jakey, and please explain to me why you are the only one in this house not wearing AirPods, forcing all of us to listen to sports replays?" *I* was even wearing AirPods in my own home at this point, and I wasn't on a phone call or listening to music; I was merely hoping no one would interact with me.

"Sorry, Chels," Jake said, and popped in an earbud that had been sitting right in front of him. The next day, the same thing happened, minus the banana split between his legs. He had retired his mesh shorts for another pair of shorts with no holes, and had also decided to put on a pair of socks. On the third day of me walking downstairs into my living room to be greeted by basketball replays blaring from his computer, I lost it.

"Hey, Miracle Ear! Put in your fucking AirPods. They look like two little balls. They shouldn't be hard for you to find."

My nephew is progressive; he understands that America was built on the backs of enslaved people, and that the world operates under a system of patriarchy and white supremacy. He understands that you need to respect women. I couldn't fathom how he could be so clueless about spreading his body around like a sea lion in a house that wasn't his own. Had he missed the years of women mansplaining what exactly the problem was and how there was a huge opportunity, whether you considered yourself guilty or not of said misogyny, to address it and be part of the solution?

Instead, he offered an explanation of how basketball worked.

I would like to go on record and say that I know only two things about basketball. One of them is that Michael Jordan is the GOAT. I know that because I saw his documentary, *The Last Dance.* You don't have to be a basketball fan to enjoy the brilliance of Michael Jordan spinning through the air making dunk shots with that thousand-watt smile on his face, winning one championship after another, completely transforming the history of sports. In his documentary, he sits in some Orange County mansion, eyes bloodshot, drinking what looks like a whiskey neat while railing on every opponent he ever faced and what an asshole that person was and is. I could not get enough of Michael Jordan. *This* was a man who had earned the right to wear mesh shorts in the middle of the afternoon. I watched that documentary eight times. The other thing I know about basketball is that the Denver Nuggets have absolutely nothing to do with chicken fingers. And now I know a third thing about basketball: I know about Caitlin Clark.

"No, Jakey. I don't want you to explain basketball to me," I said, biting my tongue. I was actively trying not to react to things that irritated me, plus I didn't have the energy to tell my nephew that I didn't know what would be more irritating: learning about a sport I have no interest in, or having him explain something to me.

We got into a pretty regular routine at my house where we would all do our own work/school thing during the day, interspersed with lunch, pool, and snack breaks, and then we would have dinner together every night, where three out of four times someone would end up crying about some dynamic that was happening in the house that hurt their feelings.

On the nights we ordered takeout, my obsessive-compulsive niece would take about thirty minutes to Windex all of our to-go food. On the other nights, Jakey would cook us one of his favorite recipes or find something new in a cookbook and "whip" that up for us. The problem with Jake's cooking was that he would start prepping around 6:00 p.m. and the food would be ready promptly at 10:00 p.m. At this point in my life, and with as much cannabis as I was consuming to tolerate my house being invaded by my family, I was in bed no later than 8:00 p.m., where I would put myself to sleep with one of the episodes of *The Last Dance.* Falling asleep with Michael Jordan became my coping mechanism to my new set of circumstances.

After two months of this, my sister Simone told me privately that she thought Jake was taking COVID and the quarantine particularly hard. She thought it might benefit him to have some one-on-one interaction with a member of the opposite sex.

"There are four of us in the house that are the opposite sex. Isn't that enough?" I asked her, perplexed.

"Not that kind of interaction."

"He wants to have sex," I asked her, "during a global pandemic?"

"Not sex," she reassured me. "They'll just sit in the backyard and follow COVID safety guidelines. They'll probably just play cards."

"Play *cards*? Like canasta?"

"I don't know, Chelsea. There's some girl he wants to meet, and let's just get out of here and give him a little privacy." I wanted to tell her Jakey should be the one to get out of *my* house and give *me* a little privacy.

"And then, when the girl leaves, he just jerks off into my pool?" I asked. "I'm confused about the run of the night's events."

"Boys are different, Chelsea. Boys need a certain amount of attention from the opposite sex. He's stressed out."

"What is he so stressed about?" I asked my sister, bewildered. "Living in my mansion? Is that stressing him out because it's certainly stressing me out, and you don't see me calling up Michael Jordan to come meet me in the backyard to play cards, because I have a *family* living with me and that would be inappropriate, *Simone.*"

The way my sister was treating my nephew was cause for concern. Mothers of men seem to be just as much of an issue as the men themselves. The coddling, the not being able to see their own children clearly, the constant excuse making for their male children. I thought my sister knew better, but it seemed once again she would need my guidance.

To add insult to injury, Simone confused my two dogs all the time, even though Bernice was half the size of her brother Bert. Simone would repeatedly ask, "Is that Bert or Bernice?" This annoyed me tremendously, especially coming from one of my siblings. As if I would ever get my niece and nephew confused.

With no fight left in me, I capitulated, and took my sister over to one of my girlfriends' houses in order to provide Jakey with some unearned private time with someone of the opposite sex.

We arrived home later that night around 11:00, and my sister and I were pretty buzzed—but not as buzzed as my nephew. He was sitting on one of the barstools at my kitchen counter with his head hung low, rubbing his hands through his hair very dramatically like he had just gotten back from Iraq. When I asked him what his problem was, he mumbled something about how frustrating it was to not be able to have physical contact with a woman. I looked over at my sister Simone, whose eyes fell to the floor in what could only be interpreted as an acknowledgment of shame. Another valuable tool I picked up in my two-year therapy stint was when to remove myself from a situation in which I knew I was close to hitting someone, so I took that moment to very gingerly make my way upstairs to my bedroom, where I sat on my balcony, lit a joint, and contemplated the future of mankind.

My sister came up to my room about fifteen minutes later and said she was sorry and that it was her job as a mother to listen to her son.

"Your *job*? It's your *job* to listen to your twenty-four-year-old son bitch and moan about how horny he is in the middle of a global pandemic, when thousands of people are dying every single day? You know who else is horny?" I asked her, pointing at my vagina. "I've been masturbating to Michael Jordan for eight weeks."

After three months of my family living with me, I decided the only clear way to send a message to my sister was to put my house on the market and downsize to a smaller property with fewer guest rooms. I wanted to send my family and any other interlopers who had any grand ideas about moving in with me a very clear message that just because I had five extra bedrooms did not mean I wanted company.

That's when they moved out. And that's precisely when I decided it was time to get down to business. I wanted to get back out there before all the single people got back out there at the same time, which would undoubtedly result in some new STD, probably called Coverpes. I needed to get ahead of that.

Through my doctor, I was able to procure an at-home Cue Health COVID testing kit. This allowed me to lure potential penetrators to my house, and when they got to my backyard gate, I would administer a nasal swab, and then go back inside the house and plug it into the cartridge that ran the diagnostics, which took about thirty minutes. This thirty minute window gave me an opportunity to interview the potential penetrator while sitting six feet apart, and if they said anything that annoyed me, or if I saw a pinkie ring, I would come back outside and tell them they had tested positive for COVID and that they needed to go straight home to quarantine for two weeks.

The array of men parading through my backyard at ninety-minute intervals was less than satisfactory. The very first guy showed up covered in tattoos and had huge muscles, which is not typically what I am looking for, nor would I consider it my "type." I have never been sure exactly what my type is, but whatever it was didn't matter. I was desperate, and I was willing to overlook things that would have been nonstarters before therapy and before the pandemic. I needed to meet the moment, and that moment was about throwing any prerequisites out the window in the name of penetration.

It was during this interview process that one man after another said something unforgivable that prevented me from being able to go the distance. One guy who wasn't a scientist, doctor, or male nurse told me he wore masks all the time, but didn't believe that they really did anything. Another guy we'll call Jack asked if his COVID test came up negative, would he be required to use a condom. The third gentleman caller of the night mentioned injuring one of his balls earlier that morning during a workout. All three of these men left my house being told they had tested positive for COVID.

I didn't understand why men were so late in getting the message about not acting like complete idiots. It was exhausting having to explain to a man in his forties that bringing up his testicle on a first date was an unacceptable and unwelcome exchange. I asked this man to recall an instance where he had been on a first, second, or even third date and had heard the term "labia." The answer was no. I asked him if he had ever heard a girl say anything along the lines of "I caught my labia on the Peloton this morning." Again, the answer was no. *Men are becoming unfuckable,* I thought.

As I sat on my deck alone reflecting on how, yet again, none of the night's candidates had cut the mustard, it occurred to me that my family's home invasion had interrupted my personal growth. I had been thrown a curveball at a delicate time in my transformation, and I had failed the test miserably by resorting to the easiest distraction possible: meaningless sex with men. This is what therapy had been like for me. Two steps forward, and then three giant steps back. I had gone a few months without Dan's guidance, and I was already floundering.

No, no, no.

Do not beat yourself up for getting thrown off course, I told myself as I inhaled and exhaled the joint I was smoking. *It's okay, this is a pandemic, you are not superhuman, you just got distracted. No self-flagellation. You're doing the right thing and you are headed in the right direction. Just keep learning and just keep growing. Pick yourself up and get back on track.*

Cuomo You Don't

Along with millions of other women, I fell head over heels in love with Andrew Cuomo during his daily COVID updates, where he would yell at all of us through the TV imploring us to wear masks and where he seemed to be the only person in the country taking control of the situation. We all had been so dehydrated for leadership, it was an easy role for Cuomo to fill, and I became extremely turned on by his authority. I spoke publicly about my crush on him one morning on *The View* over Zoom, relaying to Joy Behar and Whoopi Goldberg that I would in fact "like to be penetrated by the governor." I knew if I put my feelings out into the ether, Andrew Cuomo would hear about it.

Three days later, I got a call from an unknown number, which I did not answer, but which turned into a lengthy message from the man himself telling me he heard from a little birdie in a tree that someone had a crush on him and that someone was me.

I must have listened to that message at least sixty times on my way over to my best friend's house, where I played it for her outside her window following the six-feet-apart COVID guidelines. I held my phone up to the sky like John Cusack in *Say Anything,* while I jumped up and down yelling, "I'm going to fuck the governor!"

I called him back and we talked for about an hour while I paced back and forth in my friend's backyard. Then we started texting. I didn't want to date him, because dating a politician would definitely prohibit my own behavior, but I did want to have sex with him and tell all my friends about it.

I would watch his live press conferences every day and then search images online trying to pinpoint exactly where his nipples lived on his body. This was during "Nipplegate," when people were debating if he had a nipple piercing because something funky was definitely going on under his shirt. I knew that a man like Andrew Cuomo didn't have the guts to have a nipple piercing, but I was interested in what was happening in that department, so I spent a lot of time zooming in on his nipples. From what I could gather, it seemed like his nipples were headed in a southerly direction, and I had never faced that kind of storm before. This would be a mental and physical challenge for me, but given the affection my friends and I had developed for Andrew Cuomo during his press conferences, it became clear that it was my patriotic duty to take one for the team.

The timing was good, because my family and I had our annual summer vacation coming up in Martha's Vineyard and the house I had rented wasn't giving any refunds due to COVID. My brothers and sisters and I all agreed we should take the vacation and risk flying on planes and taking boat rides because everyone by this point had become exhausted and depressed. We needed a spirit lifter. Besides, the money had already been spent.

My plan was to go to the Vineyard for a week, shoot my HBO Max special at an outdoor venue in New York City, then head up to Albany for a little Andrew Cuomo penetration. The big hiccup here was that Mr. Cuomo stopped responding to my texts as soon as I arrived on the East Coast. I had laid out several date options for him via text because he told me he would be open to having a private dinner at the governor's mansion. And then . . . he ghosted me. My sister conjectured that someone in the governor's office got wind of our little penetration plan and put the kibosh on it in order to protect the governor from the possibility that word would get out that he was gallivanting around with a celebrity while telling everyone that they needed to stay indoors.

"This is such a bummer," I told my sisters. "I really wanted to do this for my country."

"You were probably too forward," my sister Shana told me. "Men are turned off by that."

"Even him?" I asked. "He's a governor."

"Yeah, exactly, and he probably has a big ego, and he's not used to being spoken to the way you've been talking to him. He was having fun texting with you, but once it became real, he pussed out," Shana said.

"Why don't you offer to have sex with him outside?" Simone offered. "From behind. That way, if he gets caught, he can say the two of you were as safe as possible."

I'd seen pictures of the interior of the governor's mansion, and the decor alone convinced me that sex outside would have been a more preferable option. But after he stopped texting me back, my family and I decided to have a little fun with the texts I continued to send. Shots of me on the Vineyard swimming topless while wearing a face mask; shots of me smoking a joint topless and in my underwear, with a caption that read, "It's time to legalize cannabis." I was bummed to get ghosted, but it became a delightful little game sending pictures of myself in various states of undress that might pop up on his phone or iPad and accidentally transmit to the large screen he used during daily COVID briefings, allowing the entire country to take pleasure in my shenanigans.

One night, after I had sent one of my scantily clad texts, my sister Simone and I were lying in bed at our rental house in Martha's Vineyard contemplating where life would take us. If whole sections of the country were closed down, we figured we should try to find a private beach house somewhere and rent it.

"What about Maine?" she said to me, while scrolling through her phone. "The COVID rates are low there, there's not a huge population, and they have tons of beachfront houses we could rent. Let's just build our own community."

I looked over at her phone to see what she was looking at. There were very large, very old homes on the waterfront that looked like they had been built at the turn of the century, but it was hard to tell which century.

"The furniture looks like it's from a plantation. If you and I go up there together, we are going to look like two white . . ."

". . . supremacists," she finished my sentence.

"I was going to say lesbians, but okay."

"This house is on a golf course, in a private community in Maine. It's probably very Republican," Simone informed me. "For miles."

In my indefatigable desire to reach across party lines, the idea of disrupting a Republican enclave for a couple of weeks appealed to me on a cellular level.

"Let's fucking go!"

I had already decided that this would be an adults-only vacation to wait out COVID, because by this point my nieces and nephews and their lack of gratitude for all the vacations I had provided for them was really starting to bum me out. I hadn't yet figured out how to broach this topic with my brothers and sisters, but I was becoming alarmed at the children's sense of entitlement, even though I knew I was likely the one responsible for it. I consider my nieces and nephews my children as well as my brothers' and sisters', even though I am in no way, shape, or form a parental figure. I have always felt a great sense of duty to provide for them, care for them, and be there for them. To set an example of what you can accomplish in life when you are brave enough to go after your dreams and take risks. I've always wanted to show them how to be generous and kind, not only to the people they love, but to strangers. During our Vineyard vacation, I'd realized that they were acting in ways that didn't meet these standards. I knew I had to address it, but I had to do it with love and grace instead of my old behavior of yelling, chastising, or threatening.

So, I left Martha's Vineyard to shoot my stand-up special in New York City, and before my trip to Maine, I very carefully composed a letter to all my nieces and nephews and cc'd my brothers and sisters.

To All My Nuggets

I want to start this email by telling each of you, A, B, C, D, E, F, G, and F, that I love you, for all different sorts of reasons, and that there is nothing any of you could ever do to get me to un-love you. It couldn't happen.

So, it is with great love and hope that we can use this as an opportunity to get better at being together. Our family is dysfunctional, and that is what families are. What we need to work on, however, is manners. There was a definite shortfall of manners on this trip, and I left the trip feeling embarrassed and taken advantage of.

Say hello to people who are working in the house, who are delivering something, or who work for me. You don't have to have long conversations with the housekeepers or workers, but you do need to acknowledge their existence out of decency and respect. This goes for my house in L.A., or Mallorca, the Vineyard, or wherever we happen to be vacationing. I treat my employees like family, and I expect you to do the same. Especially, in Los Angeles. They do not work for you. They work for me, and this is now a requirement.

When someone is carrying a large package or multiple boxes, whether you are a girl or a boy, I would like you to offer your assistance. Whether it be opening a door for that person, or asking to help with the food being delivered, or helping with the packages that person is carrying.

It is the nice and decent thing to do, to be conscientious of the others who are also on the vacation with you. That means not having second helpings before every person gets their first. It means not finishing bottles of Belvedere that I purchased, or ginger ale I flew with across the country, that they don't sell on the Vineyard. We must all remember that we are guests and we are not at home.

Girls—Be kind and thoughtful to my guests. Do not roll your eyes repeatedly or even, ever. My friend contributed more to this trip than anyone on this email. He carried groceries in and out; he played rugby and swam with the kids; and he spoke to each person on the trip, individually, with interest. He is my dear friend.

Do not consume copious amounts of alcohol that you did not pay for, leaving the adults with no alcohol on multiple occasions. This is never okay to do, and not a way to get invited back. I want you guys to have as much fun as possible, and that includes drinking or taking edibles or playing video games, within reason. Do not abuse this privilege again.

Clean your plates after you eat. Don't put them in the sink, and don't leave them where you ate. Open the dishwasher and put them inside.

Do not complain about food while you are eating it. This happened at every meal.

You are not at home. You are a guest.

Do not litter on the grounds of someone else's house. I rented this house from a family who built and finished it this year. They did not want to rent their house to such a large group. I called them and told them about my family and how meaningful the Vineyard is to our family, and they agreed.

It is a privilege to stay in a house so well equipped for our family. We are a large group, and it is never easy to find accommodations that fit us all. How do you think these people would react to their property being littered with beer bottles? Do you think they would rent to us again?

I understand not everyone wants to hang out with their family twenty-four seven, but I am going to require that when you are with the family, like during a game or a movie, or dinner, you are not on your phone or playing video games. You have the entire day to do whatever you want. You can make the time to be present with the family for an hour or two at night.

The best memory of this trip was when we were all playing Oval Office. Every single one of you played, and we laughed, and we had fun, and Roy had no idea what any of the answers were.

We only get those moments when we relax, and when we are present with each other. They don't happen when someone is on their phone. Moments like this are what family is and what it must remain. If you have no desire to be with your family, I can relate. I was that age once, too. But you all had fun playing that game together, when all of us were together—relaxed, and engaged. This is not required every minute of every day, but it is something I expect from each and every one of you at certain times during our vacations.

I know you are probably rolling your eyes, but I promise you, everything I'm saying will help you in life. I know your moms can drive you crazy, but you cannot speak to your mothers the way some of you do—especially not in front of other people. Save that behavior for home. It doesn't matter if we are family. It's not kind. You're only going to regret treating your moms like that. I speak from experience.

You can all help your mothers and be kinder to them when you are in a bad mood. Olga and Simone are doing everything they can to be great moms, and your moods are not their problem. They are your problem, and you are old enough to start reassessing how you want to be in this world.

A good rule of thumb as a guest is to never finish something.

When I make a pitcher of margaritas, don't finish that pitcher unless you're willing to make another.

I need everyone to say please and thank you at every opportunity, and more often.

When you see your mother cleaning, help her. I do not want my sisters cleaning dishes on their vacation. You guys can all figure out a system where you pair up with each other and take the night to load the dishwasher. While all of your mothers have no issue with cleaning up after you, I do. I'm not bringing my sisters on vacation to watch any of them do housework.

Do not come out to eat if you can't control your mood. Everyone in this family is old enough to make eye contact with restaurant workers, and every other adult you come into contact with. It is the decent and polite thing to do, and it will help you in life to be KIND to strangers, and it is now a requirement.

I want you all to know that going away with me on these trips is not guaranteed. It is a choice I make, and it is expensive. I need you guys to come to our next vacation with an attitude of contribution—not one of taking. A contribution does not mean financial. It means: What sort of pleasantness are you planning to bring on vacation? It is not a free-for-all.

I fully recognize my responsibility in this dynamic; the multiple trips where everything is planned and paid for, cleaning service every day, and just an opportunity to spoil you guys, without any boundaries or parameters. It is clear now that I have overdone it, and I hope that you are all able to see the reason and decency in these adjustments and are able to implement them.

I love you all. You are all important to me. I want to see you do better, and I promise to do better, too. I never was exposed to these kinds of vacations growing up. You are experiencing something that most people will never get to experience. I don't need you to thank me all day. I need you to show respect to the situation and appreciate it. I don't care how much our family annoys you. It's the only one we've got, and we are stuck together for life.

All my love,
Chelsea

This letter was met with some embarrassment, some anger and shock, and then apologies. The important thing for me was to relay to my family in a kind and loving way how I had been feeling for years. It felt right to send that letter. And while it didn't happen overnight, my relationship with all of my nieces and nephews has strengthened, and my entire family knows how much work, effort, and money goes into these trips. I was learning that just like my experience in therapy, change in a family dynamic doesn't happen in an instant; it happens slowly and incrementally over time, until it sticks. I had set a boundary with them, and while the initial reaction was shock, what grew out of it was a mutual respect and appreciation. This was a very meaningful development in our family dynamic, and I would never have been able to write a letter like that before therapy. I would have yelled and screamed and told them all to go fuck themselves.

So here I was: learning, reaching for better,
stepping through the prickly stuff in an effort to grow
into this woman I'd dreamed of becoming.

Maine

Simone, Shana, and I enlisted our brother Roy to join us for two weeks at our rental house in Maine, and we invited different friends who traipsed through for various lengths of time. Roy, who is a chef by profession, cooked dinner each night and we'd sit on a covered patio eating fresh fish, lobster, clams, and all the deliciousness Maine has to offer. We saw some of the most beautiful sunsets I've ever seen, laughed our asses off, took lots of bike rides into town and up and down the coast. Everyone who showed up at our house was forced to take a shower outside to wash the COVID off their bodies from whatever plane they had flown in on before they were allowed to mingle with us. Another idiotic behavioral by-product of COVID. As if you could wash a pandemic off your clothes.

I still hadn't heard back from Andrew Cuomo, so I had to accept that our little liaison was never going to come to fruition. In light of this rejection, I desired some comfort. I had a sharp longing for my dogs, Bert and Bernice. My sister found a couple who would provide the service of driving my dogs across country and deliver them to me in Maine in forty-eight hours. How anyone could drive from California to Maine in two days seemed implausible, but I tend not to ask too many questions when my desires are satisfied so imminently.

While sitting at dinner the night before the dogs were set to arrive, Roy commented that if a guy like Andrew Cuomo couldn't handle me, then he was out of ideas about men who could.

"Yes," Simone agreed. "I would have thought that would have been an almost perfect match, except for the fact you would most likely get him into political trouble whenever you spoke publicly. You'd be a huge liability."

This had in fact crossed my mind because I have a history of revealing very private things that include not only me but the men I've dated. I don't disclose these things to embarrass these men. Details and private stories have a history of flying out of my mouth before I even realize I've given away someone else's personal information. I have always been very open when telling personal stories, because I like to tell the truth. But this was one more thing I needed to work on tempering in my new life: sometimes my stories don't belong only to me, and when that's the case, it would be more considerate of others to keep my mouth stapled shut.

"Also, he doesn't drink. That would annoy you," Simone added.

She was right. That would annoy me. I had zoomed in on an Instagram picture the governor had posted of him and his three daughters having dinner. Only one of them was drinking a glass of wine, and the drink next to him looked like a Diet Coke without ice. Two strikes.

At around 8:00 the next night, an unmarried couple arrived with my dogs. I knew they were unmarried because I asked them if they were married, and the guy said, "Hell no, we're just dating, and I'm still looking."

"Charming," I told him, and then offered his girlfriend a drink.

The dogs had absolutely no reaction to being reunited with me, which I had grown used to, but having it demonstrated in front of strangers is and will always be humiliating. My dogs have never respected me, and after a while that in itself starts to feel like abuse. I wish I could write them a letter like I wrote my family. I walked back inside the house and to the kitchen, where my brother Roy was preparing dinner.

"The dogs are here," I told him, while grabbing the vodka out of the freezer. "I'm making them a cocktail."

"The dogs drink?"

"It's for the drivers. They're a couple, but not according to him. They're heading to Florida tonight."

"Don't give them more than one drink, Chels. Get them out of here after they finish that one."

"They have to be in Florida by the morning, so I don't think they're staying for too long."

My brother let out a laugh. "Yeah, I bet they do have to be there by morning."

"What is that supposed to mean?" I asked Roy. My brother turned around to look at me and lowered his reading glasses.

"Chelsea!" he said, glaring at me. "Anyone who drives from California to Maine in two days . . . is on crystal meth. People on crystal meth will rob you."

Crystal meth is one of the few drugs I have never tried, so I took what my brother said at face value. I went back outside with only one drink for the woman and told the guy that we just ran out of vodka. (I have never run out of vodka. Except when my nephews finish it all without asking.)

"I'll take a beer," the guy said. I ignored his request and chatted with the woman for a bit and then told them both thank you and sent them on their way. My disdain for men who disrespect women will never wane, and my biggest challenge when confronted with this man who drove my dogs across the country was not letting the anger consume me and instead taking joy in smiling pleasantly at him while ignoring anything he had to say.

Bert and Bernice are both rather aloof, but even taking that into account, they weren't acting like themselves. They were wandering around the property listlessly, not like dogs at all, but more like stray senile cats. Roy and I sat outside watching Bert smell a paddleboard for close to twenty minutes.

"They seem a bit off, no?" I asked Roy.

"Chelsea," he said with a sigh, taking a sip of his beer. "You just sent your dogs on a methamphetamine high-speed car chase across the country because a governor wouldn't fuck you during a global pandemic. Give it a minute. They're detoxing."

I have vast experience with drugs and alcohol, but I have never tried to push drugs on either of my dogs—even though the two of them could stand a little jolt to their systems. It's simply not the way I parent.

"This is exactly why you were right to never have children," Roy added. "Your parenting is astonishing."

I am quite sick and tired of being attacked for my lack of parenting skills.

"Oh, shut up, Roy," I snapped back, exhausted. "You try raising two dogs as a single mother on one income."

When I went to bed that night, I aligned the doggy steps—that the couple who weren't a couple brought me along with my dogs—and lured Bert and Bernice up to my bed. Then I kicked the doggy steps away so that they were both trapped because that's how I have to sleep with my family. I checked my phone to make sure Andrew Cuomo hadn't accidentally responded to any of my texts and then popped my nightly edible and drifted off.

I held Bert in my arms—not unlike one holds a lover—and detected a scent on him that was unfamiliar. *This must be what crystal meth smells like,* I thought as I fell asleep. I always knew at some point I would cross paths with crystal meth, but I never expected it to be through my dogs. *Well, at least that's behind us and my family is all under one roof.*

Maine Part Deux

For the duration of our stay in Maine, I scheduled an outdoor Pilates class every morning. After the first day, I announced that we were going to do a group meditation after Pilates every morning. We started in a circle and I turned on my Deepak Chopra app. When the twenty minutes were over and I opened my eyes, only two of my family members were left in the circle, and Roy had fallen asleep. Typical. When I checked my phone, there was a text from Barbara Bush, George W. Bush's daughter.

"Sissy!" she wrote. "I heard you're in Biddeford Pool!"

"Hi, Sissy!" I wrote back. "I am! Come say hi!" I had met the Bush sisters years ago when I was being honored at the Glamour Women of the Year awards. Since then, either they've interviewed me or I've interviewed them, and we all call each other Sissy, because when I first met them, they were together and I was with my two sisters, so it was just easier if everyone had the same name. I happened to really like both of the girls, and didn't want to hold their father's behavior against them. I wouldn't want anyone to blame me for the terrible behavior my used-car-dealer father had exhibited throughout my life, and I had come to understand that we are not responsible for our fathers' actions. If anything, we are responsible for breaking the cycle of bad behavior and treating every person with dignity and respect.

"We'll be there in five minutes," Barbara texted back. I had known when I rented the house that it was somewhere in the area of Kennebunkport, which was where the famous Bush compound is, but I never bothered to see how close they were. I hadn't even considered that either of the Bush twins would be there.

I walked from the back porch through the house to the front door in order to greet Barbara. I soon spied one Secret Service agent, Barbara, and two older women walking down the driveway.

"Sissy!" I waved, jumping up and down. "I can't believe it! What are the chances? As the two women got closer, I saw what looked like two Secret Service men walking behind them, and then I realized one of the women was the former first lady Laura Bush. *Oh, fuck,* I thought. *Too many Republicans. Thank God for COVID as a reason to stand back.*

"We should probably keep our distance," I said, smiling at everyone like a Stepford wife.

I ushered them all to follow me around the wraparound porch and to come take a look at the view from the back, which faced the ocean. We all stood admiring the view as I filled them in on how I ended up in Biddeford Pool. Laura Bush was lovely and adorable and I immediately felt all my walls crumble as I remembered she was a teacher and a mother and a human being just like everyone else. She also had dimples. I am a sucker for anyone with dimples. My brother Roy walked outside, slamming the screen door on his way out, to say hello to our new guests.

Roy instantly contradicted my COVID protocol and started hugging all three women, and when he got to Laura Bush, he stood back and said, "*You* look familiar." It was unclear if he was kidding because he seemed genuinely perplexed trying to place this woman, and we're never really sure what he knows and what he doesn't.

It was a rather brief interlude, with Barbara canoodling Bert, whose body she appreciates almost as much as I do.

"What's wrong with Bert?" she asked.

"He has a cold," I quickly shot back, before Roy could tell the former first lady that my dogs were detoxing from crystal meth.

Republican first ladies have a history of being vehemently anti-drugs and I didn't know if Laura would blame my "loose lifestyle" for the fact that my dogs were dabbling in street drugs. All my guests had gone back to their respective rooms to shower, so we agreed that Barbara and her new husband would come back to the house the next morning at 10:00 to join our Pilates class.

Pickleball was a main topic of conversation throughout this trip because my close girlfriend who was there is very involved in sports and Barbara Bush's new, very hot husband was also passionate about pickleball. I'm not passionate about anything that everyone is talking about at the same time, and it seemed as a society we were entering the dawn of pickleball. Between that and friends of mine banging on and on about Burning Man, I had found two topics that held absolutely no interest for me, which for some reason prompted people to try even harder to convert me on the subject. In my opinion, pickleball is for people who don't know how to properly exercise, and Burning Man is just a bunch of rich people sharing for the very first time. While I have plenty of friends who go to Burning Man, none of them will ever convince me that getting sandblasted while on LSD leads to a good time.

One of the mornings after Pilates, Barbara suggested that we all come over to Kennebunkport for a pickleball tournament, and it took me about three seconds to shut her down. I explained to her in no uncertain terms that it would be in no one's best interest for me to go to Kennebunkport. Forget about being seen with the former president, I explained to her that I wouldn't be able to trust myself in that situation. I have a history of outbursts and didn't want to disrespect someone in their own home. Outbursts had been a part of my personality for some time, and instead of being in denial about my own proclivities, I had learned to embrace them . . . or try to block them from happening.

"Oh, Sissy, I'll make sure Daddy is getting a massage when you come over. Don't be silly," she said.

I looked at her, looked at my friends and siblings who were all gathered on the porch post-Pilates hanging out, and saw everyone's eyes light up at the prospect of going to one of America's most famous political compounds.

"Chelsea, we all want to go to Kennebunkport. It will be fun. Don't ruin this for us," my sister Shana said.

"You're putting me in a real pickle, Sissy," I told her, as I was lying on the living room floor against a wall with my legs straight up the wall to alleviate my back, which was spasming.

Two days earlier, I had gotten stuck on a paddleboard in the middle of a tide pool and almost lost my life when I abandoned my board and swam to shore trying to avoid getting sucked into a whirlpool. I was in a sundress when this happened, because paddle boarding didn't seem any more to me like real exercise than pickleball, and the water wasn't rough enough to think otherwise. So, after swimming in circles in a whirlpool for ten minutes, with two different boats attempting to rescue me, and me waving them both off like a tough guy, I was next seen dragging my paddleboard across the rocky shore in a water-soaked sundress, looking like Nick Nolte if he had been in the movie *Blue Crush*. Any dignity that I had left was tossed into the Atlantic, where it now likely floats somewhere deep in the fjords of Norway.

"I thought after therapy you'd become more open-minded, Chelsea," my brother added.

"Not *that* open-minded," I told him. "I can't be seen vacationing with George W. Bush, Roy. It goes against everything I stand for."

"Just take an edible," Simone offered. "Or take two."

"I would take three," Roy said.

Four hours later, my sister, brother, five other friends who were staying at my house, and I pulled in to the security gates at Kennebunkport in a little caravan.

"We're not staying long," I warned everyone. "No loitering."

At this point in the vacation, I had started traveling with my own director's chair, which allowed my feet to dangle rather than putting any pressure on my spine. I had discovered through a physio in Maine that I had most likely slipped a disc during my paddle-boarding excursion, and he had directed me to either lie down with my feet up or, if I had to sit, make sure I wasn't putting pressure on my feet. I was in excruciating pain, which very serendipitously prevented me from partaking in the joys of pickleball.

Everyone had divided up into teams while I sat in my director's chair on the side of the court, with my back facing the rest of the compound. The game had barely started when I heard a very familiar voice from a few feet away and heading closer.

"I heard the funny lady was in town. Is that you?" The look on my sister's face confirmed to me that the person speaking was indeed the former president. *Fuck.*

I slowly cranked my head toward his voice, even though my back was unable to move in the same direction.

"Oh, hello there, sir," I said. "Please keep your distance for COVID purposes."

"COVID?" he asked.

"Yes," I explained. "There's a global pandemic happening right now, and while I know you guys have been holed up here in Kennebunkport, you have no idea where I just came from or what plane I just got off of."

"Okay, funny lady. Okay," he said, throwing his hands up like he had given up. Then he leaned in and said, "I know we don't agree on a lot of things, but I think we have a mutual friend. My former secretary of state has a granddaughter in comedy. You probably know her."

"I doubt it," I told him. Then my brother Roy came over and thankfully interrupted our exchange.

"Hello, I'm Roy," my brother said as he approached us with his paddle in hand. He was staring hard at the former president. "You *really* look familiar."

The way the former president paid attention to and spoke with my brother made all of my guardrails fall away. He charmed me. I found him delightful with his rakish good looks—and he had dimples, too, which helped me rationalize these new feelings, as I reminded myself that it was really Dick Cheney who was the puppet master responsible for the war in Afghanistan and the response to 9/11. This is why I could never be a politician or a juror. I would constantly change my mind based on people's dimples and good looks. The president continued to ask everyone what their relationship to me was, and he did exactly what all politicians do—he seemed genuinely interested in their answers.

His sister was standing a few feet back, and he explained that he had been on a walk with her, which he purportedly did every morning by strolling past the kitchen window of her house, and saying, "Good morning, Sissy. Are you ready to go for our morning walk?"

"Well, that's just adorable," I said, capitulating, defeated. "That's exactly why I didn't want to come here. Because now I'm attracted to you."

All I've wanted my whole life was to live on a compound with my brothers and sisters and some friends sprinkled in for good measure, and to have one of my brothers come by my kitchen window every morning to pick me up for a walk.

"Daddy, leave us alone so we can play pickleball!" Barbara yelled. I really wanted Barbara to stop referring to the former president as our daddy, but that would be a longer conversation.

Finally, he bade us all adieu and then walked away with his sister and I was grateful that the exchange had ended. I took a deep exhale, and popped another edible.

"That was a lot, Sissy," I said to Barbara.

"See, Sissy, you did great!" she replied. "All your therapy has worked!"

This was an uneasy feeling that I was having trouble digesting. I've spent my whole life saying something when I saw something, and exchanging pleasantries with someone I disagreed with on such a granular level made me feel duplicitous.

After a few games of pickleball, I decided we should cut our losses and skedaddle as quickly as possible. Sissy insisted on giving us a tour of the compound, another activity that would prolong our visit. We walked around to take a look at the view of the water with the waves crashing wildly on the rocks that buffeted the property from the Atlantic. She explained to me that each of her dad's siblings had their own house on the property, along with her grandparents and some of the other members of their family. *Goals,* I thought to myself.

"Thanks for having us over, Sissy, that was a lot of fun," I told her as we were headed over to our cars. We were almost safely out of there before I heard that familiar voice, once again, yelling, "Ms. Handler, you can't leave before taking a tour of our new house. We just had it renovated!"

I turned around and saw the man himself standing outside his front door waving for us to come inside. *Oh, God, when will this be over?* I considered reminding him about COVID again, but realized that in Kennebunkport there was no such thing. It was just brothers and sisters knocking on each other's kitchen windows going for morning walks and then afternoons of massages and pickleball. *I could get used to this,* I thought.

Roy was the first one to beeline it back toward their front door, where he dropped the director's chair he had been carrying for me. As soon as I walked in, the former president invited me to come with him to look at his artwork. "Come with me, Ms. Handler," he implored. I liked that he was referring to me as a Ms. with a hard z, as if I were one of the Golden Girls. *An unmarried hellion,* he must have thought. I walked with him to the stairwell off the kitchen where his paintings were hung, and then up a set of stairs for some more paintings, and down a short hall with more. I stopped at each one for what I thought was the appropriate amount of time, but I know as much about art as I do about *Fortnite,* which is not much. A philistine would be an apt characterization of me when I'm looking at any painting. I was at a loss. I had no idea which aspects of the painting I should comment on, and my fourth edible had seriously kicked in, so I searched high and low for a comment that would sound credible.

"The paint is so . . . *thick,*" I said, adjusting my sunglasses. The former president quickly turned his head to look at me.

"You might want to take your sunglasses off," he suggested.

"I can't," I told him, and then leaned in and whispered, "It's best that I keep my sunglasses on. Out of respect. I'm very stoned . . . on pot." His eyes widened, and a smile of recognition came over his face before we were rudely interrupted by Sissy.

"Daddy, don't make Sissy look at your paintings!" Barbara yelled, climbing the stairs in search of us. I used this as an opportunity to walk downstairs, where Laura Bush was showing all of my friends and family the renovations they had just done on their house. I sidled up next to my real sister and told her it was time to go.

"I'm having a good time," she said and walked toward George W. Bush, who was now coming down the stairs, too. "I'd love to see your art," she told him, and they turned around and went back up the stairs.

I looked at my brother Roy, who was now talking to Laura Bush. "Weren't you over our house the other day?" he asked her.

I found my friend Sophie and told her it was time to go. She told me to relax and followed Simone up the stairs to look at the president's artwork. *Jesus Christ.* My family was acting like we were at the Louvre. I decided to go back upstairs and break up the party. I interrupted my friend Sophie talking to George Bush about the Texas Rangers when I heard her bring up Colin Kaepernick. If I heard any Republican's viewpoint on Colin Kaepernick, I knew our visit would end on a sour note.

"No, thank you," I said, interrupting them. "Come on, Sophie. We have golf in an hour."

"Okay," Sophie said, understanding that I meant business. "Golf" has been a safe word of ours for years.

"We have to go, everyone!" I called out, coming down the stairs. And then I thought of something and hobbled back up the stairs to the former president.

"Dr. President!" I said, and then quickly corrected. "Mr. President, can I get a selfie with you?"

"I would love to," he responded, and then I took a picture of us.

We walked outside, where Roy retrieved my director's chair, and headed toward the cars we arrived in.

"I liked him; he's pretty charming," Simone announced.

"I liked him, too," Roy said.

"That's the problem with hanging out with these people," I warned them. "You end up liking them."

Once safely inside the car, I texted the photo of the president and me to Andrew Cuomo. I wrote, "Good enough for a president, but not good enough for a governor."

A few days later, we all packed up our things and everyone drove off to different destinations. Our Republican enclave couldn't have been more thrilled to see us go. As we were driving away, one of our neighbors, whom we'll call Karen, was standing in her driveway next to her American flag and Trump bumper sticker, waving us goodbye with a big smile on her face. I told Sophie to slow the car down, and I leaned out my window.

"Do you know how to get to Kennebunkport?" I asked. "We're late for our pickleball tournament."

Months later, Andrew Cuomo would be accused by multiple staff members of abuse of power, inappropriate behavior, and sexual misconduct, and I had no one to thank but myself for staying out of the whole thing. If I hadn't been so forward and declared what I was looking for, I could have ended up in bed with him. It seemed he preferred touching women who weren't interested in him, rather than touching women who were.

"Another bullet dodged," Shana told me when I picked up the phone the day the news broke. "That would not have been good for you to be in a relationship with Andrew Cuomo. You'd be canceled right now. I feel like Mom spends most of her time upstairs in heaven just protecting you, because it seems whenever you have the wrong inclination, someone other than you swoops in and removes the problem."

This was true. I had skirted out of many situations (not by choice) with a lot of bad characters, and this was just another example of either the universe or my mother or God having my back. I used to think people who said things like that were ridiculous. Now I understand that there are things we will never understand about the universe and what makes things happen and what makes things go away, and that your only job is to not resist reality. The quicker you accept a situation, the quicker you move through it and on from it. Let it go, and see what the universe drums up for you.

"That's how you think Mom is spending her time in heaven?" I replied to my sister. "By cockblocking me on the ground?"

"Maybe," Shana replied. "You're probably keeping Mom very busy. Why don't you cool it so she can come hang out with me?"

"Because I'm where all the action is," I reminded her.

I was grateful in the end that I hadn't gotten into it with George W. Bush. What would have been the point? I was appreciating the effects of modulating my behavior and knowing when it was unnecessary to act on an impulse. I was beginning to understand that there is a time and a place for everything and knowing when that is—and then drugging myself at times when it is important to subdue my personality.

———————————

If you are ever given the opportunity
to spend an inordinate amount of time alone,
take it. The more scared you are of being
alone, the more necessary it is to do.
Run toward yourself with open arms.
That is where your truth is waiting.

———————————

Après, Anyone?

spent the better part of my early adulthood rediscovering skiing, and I realized that it can actually be an enjoyable and less miserable experience when done on the West Coast.

A friend of mine set me up with a guy who flew me out to the Sundance Film Festival for our first date, which turned into a day of skiing. This guy was an impressive skier and he informed me when I arrived that we were meeting up with some of the Kennedys so we could all ski together. I had been skiing as an adult, but I was in no way, shape, or form ready to do any physical activities with any Kennedys.

I had hung out with the Kennedys once before: when I was in Hyannis Port, I went sailing with Ethel herself at the helm. A bunch of us jumped into the water, and a few of the men on the trip decided to "drag," which meant holding on to ropes behind the boat while it chugged through the Atlantic, their heads bobbing in and out of the ocean while they tried not to drown. I had opted out of this activity, mostly because I am sane, and also because I was on ecstasy at the time.

Instead, I got back on the boat, went downstairs to take off my wet bathing suit, and when I came back up the stairs, my dress flew up and

I ended up flashing my beaver to Ethel Kennedy. I assumed by her reaction that I would not be interacting with that family ever again, but no such luck. Suffice it to say, I knew how dangerous any sporting activity with a Kennedy could be for anyone who wasn't equipped. I expressed to my date at Sundance that while I like adventure, I was not suicidal.

When the group headed down a double black diamond run that would be better described as a cliff face, I panicked, stopped in my skis, and fell over, waiting for my date, who was already ahead of me, to turn around and check on me. When that didn't happen, I looked up the mountain to see if it was possible to climb back up and reroute. Luckily, two other people in our group had the same idea, and together we all popped our skis off and climbed to the top of the run. Then the three of us went and found a more acceptable intermediate run to ski down, and promptly found a bar for some Après. When I reunited with my "date," I very pointedly thanked him for ditching me on the top of the mountain.

"Oh, come on," he said. "Any woman worth her salt would be able to get down that mountain."

While this is the very definition of a red flag, the overarching lesson I took from the experience was not that I had to get away from this person as quickly as possible, but that I needed to become a better skier. I promised myself that after I was done with *Chelsea Lately*, I would spend an entire season paying an instructor to teach me how to ski properly, and that it seemed in my best interest to also acquire a house to go along with it.

So, that's what I did. After I quit *Chelsea Lately*, I went to Whistler for Christmas with my family, and when they left, I checked into the Four Seasons for a month. I hired an instructor whom I skied with nearly every day—who also pretty quickly transitioned into a full-time prostitute. We ended that winter going heli-skiing for the first time, and I left Whistler thinking I was the fucking boss, and that I was well on my way to becoming the professional athlete that had eclipsed me in my early adulthood. I made one of my dreams into a reality that year, and I was intent on continuing to get better and better. Skiing gave me such an adrenaline rush—even when I wasn't sleeping with the instructor—that I knew I needed to spend more time doing it.

I started spending every Christmas and birthday in Whistler, and I fell so in love with the place that when the opportunity to buy a little ski chalet presented itself, it was one of those moments in my life where I knew I had to jump. I toured the house over FaceTime in November 2020, about three days before the presidential election, and I alerted my business managers that I wanted to make an offer. Buying a place in Canada would provide me with a great escape plan in case Donald Trump was reelected, and after spending four years with him in the White House the first time, this time I was serious about leaving the country if it happened again.

My business managers can most aptly be described as Debbie Downers. They are never enthusiastic about any large sums of money I spend or donate. They argue with me about everything, working under the assumption that at any moment I could be living under a freeway. I have to repeatedly remind them that I have been in this business for twenty-plus years, and have never once been indigent, and that things always seem to come together—even though they are thoroughly irked that I never have a one- or even five-year plan.

I don't have the personality for planning, or any of the other personality traits that go along with thinking too far into the future. I mostly wait for opportunities to present themselves, or I hustle to create opportunities, and don't forget I'm half Jewish, which means I am only half-good at saving money. At one point, I was so sick of talking to my business managers on the phone I just started googling my net worth to find out how much money I had. I don't know how accurate that information is, but it's better than hearing how irresponsible I am with my own earnings.

So, I ignored my business managers' attempts to dissuade me from purchasing a house in Canada. Still, they insisted on asking what the point of the purchase was.

"To have an exit strategy," I told them.

"So, you'll move to Canada if Trump wins?"

"Maybe. I'll certainly be spending more time there than here."

"And what will you do for work?" they asked.

"I don't know. Become a ski instructor, or a bear trapper. I haven't thought that far ahead, but I'll figure something out. Maybe I'll become a Canadian news anchor."

They went on to remind me about the tax implications involved with moving to Canada, and this is when I pretended that I was getting into an elevator and hung up.

Buying a ski house was part of the vision I had for myself, and I wasn't going to let anyone talk me out of fulfilling my dreams.

"I want to be happy," I told Debbie Downer 1 and Debbie Downer 2.

"We want you to save more money for your future," they said.

"We're all going to die soon, anyway," I assured them. "I'd like to live it up before that happens."

Looking for Love?

n one of my very last sessions with my therapist Dan, he asked me what a post-therapy relationship might look like for me. Now, with the gift of self-awareness, and the understanding of what healthy compromise meant, I could be a different person in a relationship. But I wasn't sure that I was even the relationship type. I didn't see myself bending any of my habits, like eating sandwiches in bed, or skiing for three straight months a year, or taking a Xanax on a Sunday afternoon at 4:00 so I could sleep for a full fourteen hours to prepare for the coming week. At Dan's behest, I went home and wrote down a list of what I was looking for in love:

> Please bring me a man who is strong physically and emotionally. Someone who is not afraid of risk, but who also puts me in my place. Someone who values equality, and humor, and who keeps me feeling alive.

> I want a man who I can ski with, who I can travel with, and someone I can be silent with. I want a best friend.

> I want someone who is loyal to me and loyal to his friends. Someone who is willing to stick his neck out and fight for good.

I want someone brave who understands me and loves me unconditionally, and sees my mess, and loves me in spite of it.

Someone who holds me and makes me feel the way Chet did.

Someone who considers me throughout his day and is able to put my needs before his own and his before mine, when necessary.

Someone who holds my hand when we're sleeping.

I want a guy who is financially independent, but he doesn't have to be rich. I want him to have the freedom to traipse around the world with me, and the desire to make it happen.

I want someone with morals and courage.

I want a man who can challenge my thinking, who can ski like a champ, and someone who is sensitive enough to read me.

I want to connect with a man in a way I haven't yet.

Please send me someone with a great head of hair and I don't care what the color or creed. I want my match. I believe I deserve love. If you don't send him to me, I will survive, but I will remain ready for him if he comes.

Thank you.

Making the effort to write a list felt like about as much as I could muster in terms of pleading with whoever is in charge—whether it be God, the universe, or Taylor Swift—to bring me a partner. It didn't feel like *me* to write a list like that, but I understood that the old me and the new me needed to converge and that the most effective way to make that happen was to start doing things that made me uncomfortable. I had always been able to do that in my professional life, but before therapy I was loath to make myself uncomfortable in my personal life.

Dan also encouraged me to start journaling, which I doubted I would ever really do, but I did want to pick up a new habit: a type of journaling that was somewhere in between a diary and a gratitude check-in. I had definitely felt the impact of practicing gratitude for all the good fortune in my life, and to be writing down what I was grateful for seemed like an appropriate idea. I wanted there to be proof of my gratitude, just in case anyone checked.

Mountain Woman

When Trump lost the election in 2020, my faith in humanity was restored—just in time for another COVID lockdown. Spending another lockdown in Los Angeles was not on my wish list, and I was hell-bent on figuring out a way to get into Canada to spend my winter skiing. The fact that I was a new homeowner had no impact on allowing me into the country, which still had its borders closed.

So, I called my agents to ask if there was any work they could procure for me in Vancouver, which would earn me a work visa to get into the country. My longtime agent Nick Nuciforo secured me a residency at the Vogue Theatre, which would require me to perform every Saturday night. I didn't know what the hell I was going to do onstage every Saturday because I had just filmed my stand-up special and I had no new material, but I didn't care. *No problem,* I thought. I would just have to hustle and come up with an hour of new jokes.

I would be remiss not to acknowledge that millions of people were suffering during this time, losing loved ones, and trapped in their homes, and many were scared for their lives. Because of the luck and good fortune that I have been blessed with in this life, my COVID experience wasn't as dark as it was for many others. I was quite obstinate about not letting COVID get the better of me or my newly attained mental health. I was going to use the time away from people and the normalcies of life to get better at being me, to absorb all of these gifts, and to make the absolute best out of a terrible situation. I was determined to live my life out loud, even if I was all by myself.

I grabbed Bert and Bernice, filled up a plane with winter supplies, and headed to Canada with all the necessary official paperwork.

Canada was extremely strict about anyone coming in, and once you got there, there was a two-week mandatory quarantine, which would prevent me from any mingling, and which only permitted me to walk my dogs around my neighborhood. When we arrived at customs in Canada, the only questions the immigration officer asked me was if Bert and Bernice had ever been to Canada before. They had not. I chose to lie, and I told the customs officer that Bert and Bernice were a couple and that in fact they had honeymooned in Whistler years earlier, on their own. I left out the part about them being from the same litter.

"Welcome to Canada, Miss Handler, we are looking forward to your birthday ski video," the customs officer said to me.

Finally, I was with my people.

The two-week quarantine turned into another pleasant surprise. I was living in a winter wonderland where snow fell all day long. I was reading books that my home's previous owners had left for me in front of the fireplace, and trying to cook the meals my assistant in L.A. had ordered me from some online delivery service. My cooking has never yielded anything of merit and is in fact pointless, because most times I can't even bear to consume whatever I've burned or destroyed. Whatever part of the brain that allows one to follow directions is something I was born without. Or, as I've learned, I am only able to access it when I am following directions for something I care about doing properly—like skiing.

I followed the COVID rules to a T, because the last thing I wanted was to piss off any Canadians, so the only outdoor activity allowed was taking Bert and Bernice out for multiple walks a day in what seemed like their very first encounter with snow.

On one of our early morning walks, we bumped into a woman in the neighborhood wearing a huge black Canada Goose parka and some UGG boots. When she saw Bert and Bernice off leash she screamed. I looked behind me to see if there was anyone headed in our direction with a knife. There wasn't.

"What?" I asked her, scared. "What is it?"

"Why aren't they on leashes?" she said, motioning to Bert and Bernice. "Someone could think that they're *bears*." Both Bert and Bernice walk less than one mile per hour, so a leash does more to inhibit the person walking them than restrict either dog—which is why I don't use one.

I looked down at Bert and Bernice and then back at the woman.

"They're both wearing *handkerchiefs*," I said, confused. "Do you know a lot of bears that get dressed up before they go out to murder?"

Those two weeks of quarantine turned out to be a perfect time for me to start the journaling practice Dan had recommended. I was trapped at home by myself, not really doing much of anything, and each day I woke up feeling so grateful for all of it.

Arrive December 17: I feel such joy being here. This place is so cozy. My little house is so cozy, and it's small enough that I feel like I can't do anything to cause any real damage. Why have I been living in such big houses? This is so much warmer. Thank you, thank you, thank you for my life.

Day 2: Meditated for thirty minutes. Organizing day. Previous owners left their book collection for me, so I'll have to send them a thank-you note. What a nice thing to do. Had to throw away most of the pillows. The decor here is not going to work for me. There are a lot of sequins and iridescence. Did Peloton for twenty minutes. I ried to cook a chicken dish from food delivery service, but I ruined it, as usual. Got back on Peloton for fifteen minutes and weights for arms. Started reading *One Hundred Years of Solitude*.

Day 3: Meditated for thirty minutes. Better to meditate when I'm not stoned these days, better focus. Went to bed at 7:15 p.m. Wrote in the morning for two hours, trying to come up with some material for this theater residency that will be starting in two weeks. Received groceries. Took dogs out twice. They hate the snow. They also hate me. Bert is depressed about being taken away from Mabel and he blames me.

Day 4: Dogs started barking at 5:00 a.m., so I got them fed and took them for a walk, then came home and took another 33 mg edible and went back to bed until 10:30 a.m. The edibles in Canada are ridiculous. Why would anything be 33 mg? Was the coziest Sunday morning ever, but not before I heated up half a cheeseburger from last night's delivery and popped in a couple onion rings. I love going back to bed after a little snack. So cozy. Peloton for twenty-five minutes and backward squats and arms.

Day 5: Took dogs out at 6:30 a.m., have started Chopra guided meditation. They have so many courses. I fucking love it! Had deep meditation about my mother and understanding that no matter how old she got, she was always just a little girl. Read two chapters of *Letting Go*. Good to read that book and then meditate. Wrote for three hours, and think I have a new set of material that could be quasi ready for my first Saturday night in Vancouver, but I don't know how I'm going to memorize all of this in two weeks. Ugh, I really wish I didn't have to work.

Day 6: Woke up at 5:50, took dogs out, came back, smoked a joint, and scrambled some egg whites. I'm so sick of egg whites, but everything else I make is even worse. I wish I were more interested in cooking, but I just can't be bothered.

Bert keeps peeing on the carpet. It's so annoying. White vinegar neutralizes the smell. I learned that online. 9:00 a.m.—smoked a joint. Took out some garbage. The code to outdoor garbage shed was frozen so I heated up some water and poured it over to unfreeze, Bear Grylls style. Felt like I was on an episode of *Survivor*!!!! Knowing none of my friends or family can come to visit is so comforting.

Day 7: They were talking about me on Canadian television. They are pissed that I am here even though I'm quarantining. That I shouldn't be allowed to come if the lower region Canadians can't even come up to Whistler. They're not wrong, but I did follow all the rules. I got a work visa and I am quarantining. What else can I do? Peloton for thirty-one minutes. And walking lunges and some sit-ups. Made egg whites twice today. Reading *The German War*. Seventy-five million lives lost in World War II. What a waste. All because they wanted to get rid of the Jews. Seventy-five million people. For what? For hatred. When will women rule the world? Probably not in my lifetime.

Day 8: Snowed all day. Bernice is down for exploration. Bert is only down for eating snacks and being objectified. He would be perfectly happy if we never left the house and he just went to the bathroom wherever. His body is so fucking snuggly I feel I definitely favor Bert because of his body. Bernice won't let me cuddle her the way Bert does, so it's hard to give her the same amount of attention. I objectify Bert and he's down with it, and she's not, and I listen to women.

Today, I put a large pile of dark clothes in the dryer and threw a bunch of laundry detergent on it and pressed the appropriate buttons. It turns out I have been washing clothes in the dryer since I got here. It now makes sense that everything is slightly tie-dyed, and nothing is clean.

Day 9: Thursday it's been over a week. I haven't had any alcohol. I've had excessive amounts of cannabis, and my tolerance has gone through the roof. This has happened before, so I'll need to quit for a bit when quarantine is over.

Peloton for thirty-two minutes. Eight miles. Read *The German War* and cooked chicken partially baked, partially in a pan. They both tasted awful. I am learning so much about history and World War II and all the innocent lives and innocent Germans who didn't have a say in anything and were just trying to stay alive and keep their families alive, and the horror that the Jews endured. I never understood how Germans could stand by and let what happened to Jews happen, but many of them didn't know about the camps and also hated Hitler. Women need to run countries. Men are too violent. It's so hard to read about what happened to the Jewish people and the Polish people that were forced to fight for the Nazis . . . It's madness. How can there still be wars going on when we know so much better?

Day 10: Made egg whites this morning. Have to defrost outdoor garbage thingy again. Everything smells like dog food in my house now. I like this little cozy house and being stuck. I just wish I had more food, but I can't be bothered to think about what kind of food I want, so I just keep eating egg whites and peanut butter. John, the guy I was dating before I left, sent me a black dildo today, and he's not black. So that relationship is over.

Day 11: Meditated this morning for thirty minutes. One of the best meditations I've ever had. I felt the vibration of my body and then a lifting out of my body, and I wasn't even stoned. I'm not going to meditate stoned anymore. I'm getting close to something with my meditation; something is happening. I am feeling something different.

I was excited to make a toasted bagel sandwich with turkey and cheddar and olive oil and vinegar, tomatoes, mustard and mayonnaise—a recipe from my childhood—so I made it and then picked up a book about mindfulness and happened to open to a chapter about mindfulness while eating, and when I went to take another bite of my bagel, realized I had already finished it. Talk about mindlessness. I'm going to have to lay off the weed. I'm so grateful for all these books the previous owners left me. Just started *The Canterbury Tales* and *Kim* by Rudyard Kipling. Have never read either!

Day 12: Today, I disassembled a chandelier the size of a small car that was hanging over the dining room table in the shape of a giant snowflake. It was such an eyesore, I just couldn't look at it for another minute. Sat around in my ski socks and underwear in front of the fire and started a new book. I've decided to reward myself with one work of fiction before any more heavy reading, so I looked through the book selection and found *Less*. This is a book about a man named Arthur Less. Also, I love walking around my house in my underwear. This must be what it feels like to be a man.

Day 13: I got a call today that the lockdown would be extended and that the theater isn't opening until further notice, so no residency!!! I am so fucking relieved!!!! Not only do I get to be here and ski; I don't have to work!!!! People are suffering everywhere and I don't want to celebrate a lockdown, so I will just say that I am grateful for my life. I am grateful for my life. I'm going to go write that down until my hands fall off.

Update! Today, I took snow in from the deck to clean the kitchen counter, because I couldn't find the Windex. I can't seem to ever find anything when I need it. I also took a 50 mg edible just to see what happened. Not much, really. Read four hours of *One Hundred Years of Solitude*. Reading makes me so happy. I am grateful that my father forced me to read all those stupid books. I hated him for it, but I love what reading gives me. So much knowledge, so many words to look up, so many worlds to explore.

Day 14 of quarantine: Bert threw up everywhere. I threw away the comforter because I don't even know how to begin washing something like that. I took a bath, did some laundry. Read *The German War*. Did ten minutes abs and ten minutes arms Peloton class and twenty-five minutes on bike; it snowed all day, like it was raining. I love being here. I have never felt such constant joy. That's not true. I'm pretty lucky a lot, but this is other-level joyfulness, and to know I have completed my two-week quarantine and I have three months of fun in the snow. I feel so lucky. I feel grateful in a way I haven't before. This is freedom.

When my two weeks were up, I got my skis out and walked outside for my first day of fifty-five straight days of skiing. I don't remember another span of time as an adult where I would wake up every morning filled with such joy. One of the reasons I had fallen so in love with skiing was that it prevented me from being too preoccupied with anything else. When you are skiing, you have to be present and focused and pay attention in order not to die—and it turns out that focus and attention in the present moment are the biggest providers of bliss. The cold air, the trees, being outside, and the sheer rush of gunning down a mountain are pure adrenaline. Not Kennedy adrenaline, but my kind of adrenaline. My choice of adrenaline. Skiing became a metaphor for my life. The better I got at it, the more I was able to let go and let the skis do their thing.

Being in Whistler during this time felt like being on an adult spring break, and I was filling myself up with all the self-love and sustenance that comes with doing only the things you love. I'd come home from skiing, get my ski pants, boots, coat, and helmet off, grab a joint, and sit around in my underwear and ski socks reading *Little Women, The Canterbury Tales,* and a book called *A History of Canada in Ten Maps.* I read every book the previous owners left behind. I was in heaven. That winter felt like I was giving myself a giant hug and permission to be who I am. It was like I went through a tectonic emotional growth spurt. I was able to just be. To live. To be free. To not be beholden to my job or my family, or anyone. Just me and my happiness.

Skiing with the Elderly

didn't have any real friends in Whistler when I moved there for my first winter, so friends from New York and L.A. kept sending me different people to contact, because people assumed I didn't want to ski alone. I didn't have the heart to tell anyone that I wasn't looking for new friends, so when I kept getting texts from a woman named Donna who lived in Whistler, I finally relented and texted her back.

"Chelsea! Edward Shanahan told me you are here for the winter and that you need some ski buddies! We go out every morning at 7 a.m.!"

I had done a complete one-eighty in terms of being able to spend time alone, and I was beginning to worry that I was becoming a recluse. If the idea of socializing was so unappealing to me, I decided I needed to flip it and reverse it. This was my new motto: if I had a strong reaction to not doing something, I needed to do it.

"Hi," I replied to Donna. "I am free tomorrow to ski. Let me know what time you would like to meet up."

"We usually get in line at 7:30 a.m.," she replied. The mountain didn't even open until 8:30 a.m., so I didn't understand the point of getting in line so early.

"I'll text you when I get on the mountain and you can tell me where you guys are at that time."

I do get up very early, but I am not one of those people who needs first tracks on the mountain. I am not competitive when I'm skiing. I consider myself a student who is slightly scared of really good skiers—evidence of my PTSD from my date with the Kennedys. My main goal at this point was to improve my technique so that I'm never in a group that I can't keep up with. With so many Whistler winters behind me, I could definitely hold my own, but I like to take my early mornings to meditate, get all my ski gear together, make sure my gloves and socks are heated and my headphones are charged, and gather all my supplies, that is, cash, credit card, and cannabis.

We agreed to meet at the bottom of a chairlift called Seventh Heaven. When I arrived, Donna and her friend Lucy were already in line, and they were much older than I expected.

That's cute, I thought. I liked the idea of older girlfriends. Women in Whistler are tough, and just because these two were at least twenty years older than me didn't mean they wouldn't be a good time. If they skied passionately every day, it meant they were a part of the ski culture, and I love ski culture.

"Hello," Donna greeted me. "So, you're the infamous Chelsea Handler. I try not to watch TV, so I have no idea who you are."

I find this to be one of the most useless things for a person to mention to a famous person. As if that's what I'm thinking about when I meet someone: whether or not they've seen me on TV. It's such a stupid and unnecessary thing to say. The other most annoying thing to say is, "You look familiar. How would I know you? Are you famous?"

How is one meant to answer these types of questions?

"Yes, I'm famous," and then list my various television appearances? I mean, honestly. "Are you famous?" has got to be one of the most thoughtless questions to ask someone who looks familiar to you. It's just so dumb.

I assured Donna that I hadn't seen much of myself on TV either, and that watching me on television wasn't a prerequisite in any way, shape, or form for us to ski together.

"Gotta get as many runs in before the mountain gets packed," Donna declared.

"Has it been busy? I feel like COVID is keeping lots of people away. I've only really seen locals around."

The women looked at each other and laughed. "Just wait. You haven't seen anything yet."

I had been there for a month. There hadn't been one line since I showed up and I hadn't met one person who wasn't from Whistler.

"What kind of run would you like to take? Are you a beginner, intermediate, or expert?" Donna asked. Donna was the one in charge.

I don't ever really categorize myself as any of those things, so I told the women I was down for whatever they wanted to ski. Then I took one of my headphones out and put it back in the case so that I could hear music in one ear and any other necessary sounds in the other.

"You can't wear headphones when you ski," Lucy told me.

I pretended I couldn't hear her, and asked them some questions about themselves. Both women were sixty-plus years old and had been living in Whistler for years. According to them, they knew everything there was to know about the mountain. When they asked how I knew their friend Edward, who had introduced us, I explained that I had only met Edward through a friend right before I came to Whistler.

"Typical Ed," Donna said, smirking at Lucy. "Setting up his oldest friends with someone he barely knows."

"Anyone want a hit of a vape?" I asked, pulling out my pen, once we were situated on the chairlift.

"No, thank you," Lucy replied, with a small dose of hostility.

"A lot of people aren't happy you are in Canada," Donna informed me. "I would try and stay undercover if you don't want any trouble."

"Thank you," I said. "That's nice information to have."

It felt like I was being bullied on a chairlift at the age of forty-four. I couldn't help but smile and think of how ridiculous this entire situation was. I didn't want to ski with these women in the first place, but because I am very serious in my life about follow-through, I did, and was now being treated like an annoying third wheel who was cramping their style, one they were embarrassed to be seen with. *Absolutely absurd.*

When we reached the top of the lift, Lucy and Donna hightailed it off the chair and traversed over to the run like some sort of elderly Olympic athletes. Once at the run, Donna yelled back in my direction. "Try and keep up!"

They took off like two bats out of hell and left me in the dust. I turned my music up louder and headed after them. They were fast, and I needed to step it up. I was determined not to let two women in their late sixties beat me. I gained some speed and made some quick turns in an attempt to go faster, but when I realized I wasn't getting closer, I decided to straight line it in order to catch them. I held on for dear life. As I was gaining on them, Donna looked over her shoulder and caught that I was getting closer, and then really stepped on it. She beat me to the bottom.

"You girls don't mess around," I said, when I finally caught up to them at the lift line. I wanted to assure them that I wasn't a threat, because it felt a lot like I was being hazed.

"We moved to Whistler to ski, and that's what we do, isn't that right, Lucy?" Donna replied as more of a statement than a question.

"Okay, but are we racing?" I asked Donna. It was obvious at that point that Donna was the alpha and Lucy didn't have much personality of her own.

"Well, if you can't keep up, we can slow down," Donna said. I felt like I was rushing a sorority and I wasn't going to get accepted.

"No, I can keep up," I assured them.

The next run, the two of them took off like two bats out of hell, once again. This time, I wasn't having it. I gunned it down the mountain as fast as I could and was just about to pass them when I thought to myself, *What in the fuck are you doing? You do realize that what you are choosing in this moment is to race two sixty-seven-year-old women down a ski hill?*

In that exact moment, Donna wiped out and started tomahawking down the mountain. It lasted for a good minute and a half. When she finally came to a stop, Lucy and I both skied up to her to make sure she was okay and to offer to help. She was embarrassed and brushed us away.

"I never fall," she repeated over and over again, looking at me as if it was somehow my fault that she had wiped out.

Once I realized she wasn't hurt, I couldn't help myself.

"Maybe you should slow down. You were really out of control." Her hostility and eagerness to school me on the slopes ricocheted right back in her lap when she wiped out. It was comforting to see karma work in real time.

After a few more runs, the ladies mentioned we'd be going in for lunch, and informed me that they had packed their own. They walked into the main cafeteria and looked around for an open table. I haven't worked my entire adult life to eat in a ski mountain cafeteria, or to pack a lunch. I like nice things, and I like margaritas, and I was definitely not vibing with these two.

"I like to have a margarita at lunch," I told them.

"The only place to get a margarita here is at Christine's and they don't take walk-ins, and it's nearly impossible to get a reservation," Lucy informed me in a very patronizing tone that she had learned from following Donna around.

"Oh, I already have one," I said, smiling, enjoying that moment. "It was really nice meeting you two." Then, with an extra pep in my step, I sauntered over to my favorite restaurant on the mountain and sat down by myself and ordered a margarita. I consider being in my company of high value and wasn't going to waste my vibes on two boner killers. At lunch, I fantasized about setting Donna and Lucy up with my business managers

I sat pondering the idea of women that age bullying someone my age and wondered what their problem was. Was it because I was famous and they assumed I was full of myself? Was it because they were unhappy about their own lives? Did they feel threatened by me? What are the reasons women treat other women with such lightly veiled contempt? Why would women in their sixties be filled with such insecurity? What is the point of growing older if you don't get better at dishing out love and kindness?

I'm not sure what's going on with women who aren't champions to all women. But I also know that it's not my problem to figure out. The people who don't get you are not your problem. Sitting around and thinking of all the people who don't love you or don't want to hang out with you diminishes your own light. Focus on where the light and love come from and park yourself in front of that. There are many moments in life when your own light is all you need.

As I sipped on my margarita, I promised myself as an adult woman in my forties I was not going to ever make another woman feel unwelcome, and I was certainly never going to invite another person to do something with me and then treat them badly, or compete with them. I thought back to my childhood where I bounced from one elementary school to another making friends with the first girls I met, whether they were nice or not, just so that I had some people to sit with at lunch. That wasn't who I was anymore. I was confident, happy, and secure being on my own. Just because I had no friends in Whistler didn't mean I was desperate enough to take anyone. I wasn't going to let those women rain on my parade. I was at a place where I didn't need everyone to like me, and I didn't need to people please. I was now in the business of pleasing myself. I had worked so hard to get here; my wish is for all women to hold themselves in such high regard.

The next day, I hired a ski guide to take me skiing a couple days a week, and I was looking forward to using those lessons to keep improving. I figured I'd spend the rest of my days alone on the mountain. I thought it in my best interest to hire a woman this time, due to previous bouts of sleeping with more than one ski instructor. I have a tendency to become attracted to any man in charge of my well-being, whether it be a doctor, anesthesiologist, or white-water rafting guide. This is not an uncommon occurrence for women who have been neglected during their childhoods. The idea of a man in charge focusing solely on my well-being is definitely a turn-on. The only way for me to avoid these feelings is to hire women, so that's what I did.

Angela Shoniker

t wasn't long after I moved into my house in Whistler that I made a good friend there: Ange. Her husband, Ben, runs the VIP service that had taken care of me and my family for years. Due to this relationship, and my new part-time residency, Ange felt a sense of responsibility toward me. She wanted to make sure I had a community. She would show up at my house most mornings to ski with me, and then she slowly started introducing me to all of her friends.

Ange is shaped like a garden gnome. She is a little ball of muscle, because she runs anywhere from five to twenty miles per day. She is always on the move, whether it be running, biking, skiing, or running around in circles in her own kitchen preparing food for her entire neighborhood. She is a person who exercises like her life depends on it. She will show up at Après, dance on tables, and take her top off with little provocation. She does this less now because she has two children, and they have asked her to stop taking her top off, but she still does it. The whole town knows her because at various points throughout the day she has run by them on foot in the sun, rain, or snow.

She runs marathons with a month's notice; she's done triathlons, even though she is scared of the water. She has done half Ironmans, and other competitions that test your strength, stamina, and sheer determination. This woman is capable of almost any physical activity. She also spends her days managing multiple rental units and has, on more than one occasion, cleaned one or two units for new renters before she comes out skiing. She has cleaned my house and moved my furniture, and she could definitely carry my body if needed, even though she is only five feet two.

When you ski with Ange, you ski behind Ange because she is always way ahead of everyone else finding some scary shit. Somehow, we always make it back home safely, even though there have been some very questionable descents.

On any given afternoon, you will find all the kids in her neighborhood over at her house, and she regularly cooks dinner for eight to twenty neighborhood kids.

She can do anything. Except maybe stand-up comedy. That would be a disaster.

She also has a temper, a fuse, and will go off on someone at a moment's notice. I have never been a victim of one of the outbursts, but I know that day is coming. She has outbursts the way I used to have them before therapy, and she loses it on people mostly due to their incompetence, slowness, or laziness. Sometimes, when she's yelling at people, I feel like she is yelling for all of us. She's an ally for anyone with anger.

In her defense, she does apologize for these outbursts to whomever she has reamed, and if you are a good enough friend, you understand that she juggles more than most and takes on more than she should, which causes her to completely lose her shit once a week. Personally, I find it quite entertaining.

Many people who meet Ange are overwhelmed by her level of energy. They say she's "a lot." I say to those people: it's better to be a lot than to be a little. However, Ange is both of those things. She is "a lot," and also very little.

Feb 25: Had a great birthday today. Skied in a blizzard and my house was filled with flowers when I got home. Ange came over with all her wild energy and it reminded me how lucky I am. Am so grateful I started writing down what I was grateful for. It changes your vibe, and I'm grateful to have learned about gratitude.

This past winter, Ange went heli-skiing, when one of the men she was skiing with got caught in an avalanche and was buried. They were all experienced skiers, so the man had a strong chance of being rescued, but I knew as soon as I heard about it that the first person to the scene would be Ange, and it was. She hiked up the mountain with her skis on faster than everyone else and whipped out her transceiver to try to locate the body. When she did, she started digging and she was the first person to hit the guy's helmet with her shovel. She helped rescue someone from an avalanche. She saved someone's life.

I was so proud of her that day. There wasn't a chance that anyone was going to be buried in an avalanche when Ange was on the scene. That's how dependable she is. How capable. Some people are just more capable than others, and it's a beautiful thing to see.

Poopsie, Whoopsie, and Oopsie

Awhile ago, I dated a man who was divorced with three daughters, ages eight, nine, and seventeen. My boyfriend and his ex-wife both traveled around the world for their respective jobs, and the kids spent a lot of time bouncing between each parent's home in Los Angeles, with the bulk of the supervision being delegated to the seventeen-year-old.

I made it clear to this man that there was absolutely no reason for me to meet his children unless things between us became serious. As it stood, because of his schedule and mine, we didn't see that much of each other to begin with, and I didn't want to complicate things further. His response was that his kids were basically self-sufficient adults and that they could handle meeting me at any time. After all, he and his wife had been divorced for years and had a very amicable relationship, and they wanted their kids to be *of* the world, not just in it. What that had to do with me meeting them was unclear.

We had been dating for about two months when, on a late afternoon on Valentine's Day, all three girls showed up at his house in Santa Monica. He wasn't even home at the time.

My first instinct was, of course, to flee the scene. But when I saw his two youngest girls looking at me with big round eyes that revealed a kind of sadness, mixed with some disappointment in discovering their father wasn't home, and some excitement about meeting me, I recognized something that reminded me of my own youth. I, too, had yearned to be seen. I, too, was easily disappointed. And I, too, had been so easily pleased. Childhood pain recognizing childhood pain. These girls needed attention, and I knew that desire like I knew the smell of my brother's flannel shirts, the ones I used to sit in his closet and sniff months after he died.

Additionally, my personal experience makes me extra sensitive to threes. I come from a family of threes. Three boys and three girls. My mom also came from a family of three girls. Her sister has three daughters, who also have three daughters between them. My two sisters have three daughters between them. There are many boys in all parts of our families, but it is the women who are the glue, who run the show, who are the matriarchs. Even though we are outnumbered overall by men, there has never been a patriarch, except for the women in our family. When I see three sisters together, I want to jump in and join them, and I want to remind them that it is up to them to keep the family together.

"Happy Valentine's Day!" I announced, feigning as much enthusiasm as I could for a holiday I don't care at all about.

At this, the oldest one's eyes filled with tears, and then she stormed outside to the terrace.

"Oopsie whoopsie," I said to the two younger daughters, who were standing in the foyer staring at me, waiting for my next move. When I said this, they let out a howl of laughter, so I took the opportunity to explain to them that I had a cat growing up called "Poopsie Whoopsie," and whenever the cat went to the bathroom in our house, we would say, "Poopsie Whoopsie had an oopsie."

Much to my delight, the girls thought this was hysterical. They started repeating, "Poopsie Whoopsie had an oopsie," back and forth to each other until they were laughing uncontrollably. Their reaction was working in my favor, so I also started laughing, even though I wasn't really clear exactly what I was laughing about. Now I had two happy girls in the kitchen, and the older one outside on the balcony, crying. There were no other adults in this scenario and whatever maternal instinct I like to pretend I wasn't born with kicked me right in the gut, so I walked outside to check on the oldest.

It was the same instinct I had when my sister and I took her daughter to a play at the Paper Mill Playhouse in New Jersey. At some point during the play, the fire alarm started blaring. I grabbed my two-year-old niece, held her close to my chest, and was one of the first evacuees to get outside. When my sister Simone appeared moments later, her hands were thrown up and she was shaking her head.

"What the fuck was that?" she asked me, grabbing my niece out of my hands. "You take my baby, and leave her mother and *your* sister inside? Are you planning on raising her after her mother dies in a fire?"

I hadn't thought about any of that, because I had been overtaken by an urge to protect the baby—the most helpless of all of us—and in that moment I realized that a maternal instinct doesn't skip certain women, all they can do is choose to ignore it.

"My dad and I were supposed to go out for Valentine's Day tonight. Just us," my ex's oldest daughter said, as I approached her on the balcony.

I wondered what on earth my boyfriend had been thinking when he left that morning and told me to be ready for dinner by 7:30 that night, omitting any mention that his girls would be arriving.

"My dad does this every year. He promises he'll take me out for Valentine's Day, and then he forgets and instead spends it with whatever girlfriend he has at the time."

I was disgusted by my boyfriend in that moment. Not because he had different women passing through his life on a regular basis, and that I was just another one, but because his daughter seemed so broken, so resigned to the many ways he'd disappointed her.

She was beautiful but didn't know it, she was extremely shy, and there was a quiet sadness about her.

I wasn't going to leave her in that state, and I wanted to give her some sign that I wasn't ever going to take her father away from her, or come between them, or any of the things I was sensing she was thinking. I assured her that if her dad told her they were going to have Valentine's dinner together, then that was what was going to happen, and that I would make sure of it.

When I got around to calling my boyfriend, he admitted he had completely forgotten that his ex was going out of town and that the girls would be spending the week with him. He and I had dinner plans for the evening that did not include any of his daughters, so I quickly suggested he pivot and take his oldest daughter to dinner without me.

"Absolutely not. They are children and they are not going to dictate how I live my life."

I remember flinching upon hearing that, a distasteful sentence coming from someone I was falling in love with. There is nothing quite as disappointing as hearing a man dismiss his parental obligations.

He then suggested that we instead take them out for ice cream after our dinner, or even easier, we could bring home some dessert. They were just kids after all. They didn't need to go out with us on Valentine's Day.

I told him in no uncertain terms that we would not be going out together on this Valentine's; he was going to take his oldest daughter to the dinner he had planned for us, and I would stay home with the two younger daughters and figure something else out for their Valentine's Day. I reiterated that he had a very sad seventeen-year-old who wanted to spend time with her father, and I reminded him that he had less than a year before she went to college to make sure she felt less disappointed and more loved. It wasn't an ultimatum, but it was an ultimatum, and he heard me. I come from a family that wants to spend time together, and it became clear rather quickly that I could be useful in demonstrating that philosophy to this family.

I walked outside and told his oldest daughter that she and her dad were in fact going to dinner, and then I told her we had been planning this as a surprise for her all along. Those eyes of hers brightened and the look on her face was one of gratitude, love, and feeling seen. I saw her and she saw me see her, and then she wiped her tears away. I wanted to reach out and put my arms around her, but I resisted the urge, wanting to be tactful about how I proceeded.

"Okay, now let's get you ready for dinner," I said, and we walked back inside to find her two younger sisters running around the kitchen yelling at each other. "I'm Poopsie, and you're Whoopsie!" the nine-year-old yelled to the eight-year-old, chasing her around the kitchen.

"No, I'm Oopsie," she shot back at her older sister. "The youngest is always an Oopsie."

"She's right," I told them both. "I'm the youngest. The youngest is always an Oopsie."

"I want to be Whoopsie," shouted the nine-year-old.

I turned to the oldest one, whose frown had turned upside down and whose eyes were dancing with delight at her sisters yelling back and forth to each other, "Poopsie, Whoopsie, Oopsie."

I caught her up to speed, and then she declared, "As the oldest, I will be Poopsie." Then she pointed to her nine-year-old sister and announced that she would be "Whoopsie," and the youngest, of course, would be "Oopsie."

"And there it is, girls," I said. "She's the oldest and she makes all the decisions. Now, I'm going to have to remember who's who," I yelled as I started chasing them around the kitchen island. I didn't really know what I was doing or which direction our evening was headed, but I jumped aboard and thought, *While I am the captain of this ship, I'm going to make sure they are experiencing joy.*

And so it began.

.   .   .

When my boyfriend came home, he found his three daughters and me in the bathroom getting Poopsie ready for her big night out. It felt like we were getting her ready for the prom. We all helped with hair and makeup and picking out the perfect dress. As soon as they saw him, they all ran toward him.

"I'm Oopsie, she's Whoopsie, and that's Poopsie," the youngest declared, pointing at her oldest sister.

I stayed home that night with the two younger girls, and we talked and ordered in food from two different places because they both wanted different things and it was Valentine's Day.

Whoopsie and Oopsie were quite the combo. They peppered me with one question after another. They wanted to know why I didn't have my own children, why I liked their father, if I went to work every day, and if I knew that I was going bald, or that I looked like a man from certain angles. Then they put different Snapchat filters over my face to make me look obese, give me purple hair, or give me some version of a face enveloped in what appeared to be . . . a scrotum? Then they both pulled on my hair to see if it would come out because it was so "thin." The whole experience was brutal.

The youngest, Oopsie, was calmer and sweeter, and more snuggly than her older sister Whoopsie. Whoopsie was the middle child, and she was intent on making sure I knew she was the one in charge of her little sister, and that she was also the funny one, and that at nine years old, she was a force to be reckoned with. She was signaling to me that it would be in my best interest to not push back. While Oopsie was sweet, affectionate, and still very much a little girl, Whoopsie highlighted the massive difference there is between the ages of eight and nine.

The only children I had spent any real time around were my nieces and nephews, but with them my role is pure aunt. I provide fun and entertainment, and when life's serious problems come their way, I am nowhere to be found. With these girls, my role didn't feel like an aunt, or even a sister. It felt parental, and protective.

The next morning, my boyfriend was in the kitchen making all five of us pancakes. He had changed his tune rather quickly and was very attentive to all three girls. He was present with them, he sat with them and joked with them, and it was quite refreshing to see. He just needed a little reminder, I assured myself.

This dynamic continued for the next few weeks. It seemed now that I had met his kids, there was no reason they shouldn't be around all the time when their mother was out of town. I found out there were many times in which their mother had been out of town, when they chose to stay at her house alone, because their father was always working, so what was the point in going to his house, anyway?

I didn't think that sounded appropriate for two young girls. Poopsie, the oldest, had a life of her own, and was bouncing from one high school party to another. She was hard to pin down and had a floating-like quality when she was around. Almost like being in a dream state. She'd always come say hello, and tell me a thing or two about a boy or a friend, and then she'd hide out in her room until she went out at night. I tried hard with her, but made very little progress in getting to know her better.

One night, I asked if she wanted to come out to dinner with her father and me, just her. For an "adults only" dinner.

"You mean so I can be ignored?" she asked.

The disengagement between my boyfriend and his girls was obvious, especially with the oldest. She needed her dad, and he was not showing up for her. He didn't seem to grasp the importance of what was happening in these girls' lives and that in order to properly parent, he would have to become less obsessed with work, and step it the fuck up.

Before our dinner that night, I took a long walk with him and made sure he knew how important it was to make his daughter feel special, and that she, specifically out of the three girls, was the one who needed his attention most. She was about to go off to college, and without a healthy loving relationship with her own father, she was going to look for what she was missing with him in other men. Did he want to send her out in the world like that?

After that, he and Poopsie started spending every Thursday night together, doing something of her choosing. They'd go to a play or a bookstore, or a concert, and every time they'd come home, Poopsie was walking taller and more confident. She loved this time with her dad, and it seemed to be rubbing off on him as well. He was lighter, less serious all the time, and was able to put his phone and work away for small windows of time at night and on the weekends.

About a month after Valentine's Day, I got a text from my boyfriend's ex-wife asking me if I would be able to join the girls and their father on spring break. She said that Poopsie already had plans to go away with a friend from school, so it would only be the two younger girls on vacation. When I told her that I hadn't been planning on joining them in the Bahamas, she asked if she could call me. During my conversation with her, she made it clear that my presence was having an impact on the girls and their relationship with their dad. She said that she and the girls would all feel better if I went with them on spring break. Without my presence, it was likely my boyfriend would become distracted with work, as had been his pattern in the past.

Am I the nanny now? I wondered.

I forwarded the text to my sister Simone.

"Are you the nanny now?" she asked.

Reading between the lines, and applying whatever knowledge I had already picked up by dating this man, I thought the problem was pretty obvious. Their father was a workaholic who believed his girls had asked to be born, and other than being financially responsible for them, they were on their own. Their mom, an incredible woman, had a huge job that took her out of the country many months of the year. They both had this very removed way of looking at parenting. Their lives and jobs were not to be impacted by having three children, and the children were expected to understand this, however harsh that seemed. These were adults with full lives—who also had children. Not adults with children—who also had full lives.

This was all occurring when I was between gigs, so, with my time off, I decided to step in and help them both step it up. I felt a keen sense of responsibility and value at being asked to go on the trip, not only by the adults, but by the kids. I felt needed, and I liked that. It felt like I was making a contribution.

So, off we went to the Bahamas for one week.

At this point in their lives, Whoopsie and Oopsie were two very large handfuls of prepubescent innocence, drama, laughter, love, and nudity. Whoopsie was louder and more mercurial, so she could flip on a dime, and it would be unclear as to what had set her off. But because I recognized so much of myself in her, I had the patience for her mood swings and was better than anyone else at turning her around. Or maybe, it was simply because no one else had ever tried.

Whoopsie and Oopsie were still holding on to the remnants of their childhood chubbiness and they'd strip their clothes off the minute they walked into the hotel suite we were all sharing.

"Uh, girls, you both need to put some clothes on," I told them, when I walked in the door and spotted them chasing each other around the living room on Rollerblades . . . nude. "Chels, come in the hot tub with us!" Oopsie screamed.

"Girls," I said, "you need to put some clothes on." I didn't like the optics of having two underage girls roller blading around with all their body meat exposed and me being the only adult on-site.

"You are both minors, and I definitely can't be *naked* around minors," I explained. The girls thought this was the next funniest thing they'd ever heard. They started chanting, in the tone of a cheer for a high school football game, "Stop! Stop! Don't touch me there. This is"—pointing at their respective peekachus—"my no-no square!" I couldn't believe they were mocking *me* for my prudishness.

Then they both barreled over to me and started attacking me, ripping off my clothing. Even though they were only eight and nine, they seemed larger and stronger than me. Luckily, I had just come back from a hike and was wearing multiple layers that staved off the assault. Finally, I got serious.

"Girls. Stop it. You can't take my clothes off. It is not appropriate. You both need to put bathing suits on, and then I will come in the hot tub with you. The three of us naked together is not legal!"

It was hard to say all of this with a straight face, but I knew I was the only adult in this situation and that I had to set a boundary. The girls looked at each other shocked at my tone, and roller bladed back to their room to find bathing suits. Watching their tushies scramble away butt cheek to butt cheek, it was hard to restrain myself from physically attacking their naked meat, but I know that adults aren't allowed to touch children in such a manner.

Moments later, we were all in bathing suits sitting around the hot tub when one of the girls said, "Chels, we've never seen you get mad at us. You're like the father we've never had."

There it was. Out loud.

"I can't be your father," I told them. "You already have one."

"Well, you definitely can't be a stepmother," Whoopsie said. "They're the worst."

"I wouldn't mind being a *stepfather*," I said. "That feels like something I could crush."

"But then would you have to marry our mom?" Oopsie asked. "So, we could all be together?"

"I like 'stepfather,'" Whoopsie announced. "These are modern times. There's no reason you can't be our stepfather."

"'Stepfather' it is," I said, smiling.

"'Father' for short," Whoopsie said. "We call our dad Dad, so you can be 'Father.'"

"Oh, Father," Oopsie exclaimed. "Come over here so we can rip your bathing suit off, and get you naked!"

"No!!!" I yelled, getting out of the hot tub and running down the steps onto the lawn. We did this for hours. They'd chase me through the gardens of our hotel, and then I'd flip it and reverse it and start screaming like a lunatic while chasing them around the grounds. I'd pretend I was off my rocker and run through bushes, flower beds, screaming, "A dingo ate my baby!"

The rest of the trip was me and the two girls, spending our days at the beach, or on snorkel trips, or me sitting at the pool filming the two of them doing dances. They tried to rope me into making a dance video, but once they caught wind of how bad my dancing is, they were so embarrassed for me they pretended the dance worked better with two people instead of three. Their real father had checked out early on the trip due to a work emergency, and I can't say that any of us even noticed. He became almost like a third wheel. He'd come to dinner and the girls and I had all these private jokes, and he'd just sit there, left out and confused. Then they'd say "Father" and we would both look up.

I was having a blast playing the role of stepfather, because all it required of me was spoiling the girls rotten with fun dinners out, shopping trips, tickling them in inappropriate places, and lots of fun adventures. It gave me the utmost pleasure to step in and help out with all the extra love and attention these girls were craving—and that filled me up with a whole bunch of love and purpose. The pressure of full-time parenting was off, and I was able to show up for these girls in a way that gave me a lot of joy. Joy was something I experienced daily and in large quantities whenever I was around the girls.

Their dad had been bouncing around the world for years, passing them back and forth, leaving the girls to wonder about whose priority they were. They were dehydrated for attention and love, and I could think of no better objects for my affection. I had always thought I'd make a great stepparent, and here I was stepparenting my way into their lives and hearts and getting so much ridiculous fun and purpose from it. It made me feel good that they always wanted my attention and wanted to be with me. I remembered what being eight and nine was like and I wanted them to know they had an ally in me, and that I would be there for them, helping their parents out and becoming someone they could count on.

They taught me all about the latest technology I had no interest in learning about. They showed me how to mute, delete, block any unwanted engagement online. They demonstrated that you can check and see if someone had received or read your message and at what time. All sorts of options I had no idea existed that seemed so damaging to the human adolescent psyche. Is it not enough to know that someone didn't respond to your text; must we look and actually see the time they read it, right before they chose to ignore it? No, thanks. I don't have the energy for that many steps, anyway. I usually lose interest in anything after the second step.

I'd sit and play games and watch their favorite YouTubers with them, and snuggle with them nonstop. After we played some game that involved spelling, I was alerted to how terrible their spelling was. By nine years old, I certainly knew the difference between "their" and "there." So, I started creating fun spelling games where they would have to compete against each other to see who could spell something faster. It worked, because they'd ask me to play that game all the time, and there were always silly prizes for the winner.

They would take turns sleeping in my bed, insisting I tickle their back until they fall asleep, usually leading me to fall asleep first, and then being woken up, only to be told to continue scratching their back because they were not asleep yet. Several nights, my boyfriend ended up in one of their bedrooms, because both girls would crash in bed with me.

When we got back to L.A., I bought them the entire Sweet Valley High series, and impressed upon them how important reading books is. I'd chase them around the house trying to get their neck meat and then tickle them uncontrollably. Then they would fight over who got to sleep in my bed each night, when their dad was out of town.

"I want to sleep with Father," Whoopsie would tell Oopsie.

"You slept with her last night. It's my turn," Oopsie would reply.

Because I had taken most of the year off, and had a lot of free time, I started dropping off and picking up the girls from dance class, soccer, and whatever other activities they busied themselves with. I wanted to give the oldest one a break from all her responsibilities. She needed her own independence, the space to enjoy her life without the responsibilities that come with parenting. I had officially turned into someone who was carpooling children around town; I was a regular Mrs. Doubtfire, and I felt immense joy and pride in this new role.

By the end of the school year, Poopsie was having dinner with us more and spending a little more time at home. Mostly, because her dad was becoming more available, and since that was the person whose attention she really craved, she freed herself up for him. When, at the end of her senior year, she asked me to take her shopping for a prom dress, I made her dad come with us.

We spent hours together at the Century City mall and some other stores on Melrose, and when her dad walked away on one of his work calls, she confided in me just how distant she and her dad had become. He had a long-term girlfriend prior to me with whom Poopsie had a difficult relationship. Someone she felt was competing with her for her father's attention. If this were any other teenager, my first thought would have been I was being manipulated, but Poopsie wasn't like that. She was without guile, not a mean bone in her body. Quite loving, very thoughtful and caring, not spoiled at all like so many L.A. kids, and most important, she had a very soft heart that I could sense had been repeatedly bruised.

I loved this time in my life because it felt like I was really giving. It felt so good to spoil these girls. It felt important to be helping them have a better relationship with their father. I saw both my boyfriend and his ex juggling all their travel and careers, with the end result being neglect of their children. I had the time and energy necessary to step in and lighten their load, and I saw so much of myself in the girls. The adolescent frustration and anger, the insecure feelings of not belonging. The hurt that comes along with being young. The three of them coming into my life couldn't have happened at a better time. I was available and I took my new parenting role very seriously.

And then my boyfriend and I broke up. The love that I had felt for him in the beginning had transferred to the girls. I loved them, but I no longer loved him.

This was just at the beginning of my therapy, so what was supposed to be a closing conversation turned into a screaming match, and it all became very ugly. We had been together for almost a year, and during that time I had bonded with the girls, and in our breakup he accused me of abandoning them. He wanted me to explain to them why I was leaving; otherwise he would take the blame the way he had taken it for everything else.

I didn't think that sounded right. Breaking up with the girls sounded like a possibly traumatizing, unnecessary act. When he pressed me on this, I reached out to a parenting specialist I had seen on Instagram to seek counsel on what the best approach would be. She explained to me that girls their age do not need to bear the brunt of a breakup or their parents' emotions, and that burdening them with a conversation like that would be unfair. We weren't divorcing, she said. We were just breaking up and kids are resilient and they'd get over it. I felt like this advice sounded a bit cold, considering all the time I had spent with the girls, but I also felt that deferring to a professional was a much better avenue than trusting my own parenting instincts.

I have never been good about boundaries—drawing them or respecting them. This was another example of me having overstepped, gotten enmeshed in the girls' lives, and now I wanted out, and the fallout would be messy.

I hadn't yet gleaned the ability to separate instinct from action, so when I went to speak to my boyfriend about all of this, I ended up just reading him the riot act about what a terrible father he was. I told him everything I had been thinking for months. I said things I will never be able to unsay, and I let him know that his girls had been neglected—by him—and that his lack of interest in them, and lack of accountability for his own parenting, were damaging his daughters. I believe I ended our conversation by saying, "You have got to be one of the most selfish men I have ever met, and I hope your daughters never end up with a guy like you."

I figured Poopsie was old enough to handle an adult conversation, and after all she had shared with me, I didn't want to seem like one more person in her life who was abandoning her. I sent her an email explaining that her father and I had broken up and that I was always available for anything at all, if she so desired. I told her how much I admired her, how much she meant to me, and that she would always be my firstborn. That had been our joke throughout our relationship—that I was actually their birth father. She never responded. I ignored my own instincts and listened to the parenting coach, so I never had a conversation about the breakup with the younger girls.

Three weeks later, my ex-boyfriend's ex-wife called me to ask if there was any way I could spend even an afternoon with the two younger girls. She said that they missed me and didn't understand my absence. They had been through a steady stream of their father's girlfriends and had been disappointed multiple times. She asked if there was any way I could go watch Whoopsie's soccer match at school, or maybe show up to Oopsie's Spring Sing.

I forwarded the text to my sister Simone.

She wrote back saying that it seemed like the girls really needed someone to show up, that even though it was definitely not my responsibility, it would probably make Whoopsie's and Oopsie's day if I went to see them. She told me if I had the time, it would be a worth-while endeavor. To not think of my ex, but to do it out of grace, as a favor to some children. After all, if I was never going to be an actual parent, the least I could do was help out once in a while with other people's kids.

I went to both the soccer game and the Spring Sing. The girls' reac-tion to my presence made me feel like I was saving the planet. I had never felt more purposeful than I did in the moment Oopsie got off the stage after singing her solo. She was about to sit down with the rest of her classmates when she saw me standing in the back of the audito-rium. Her face lit up like the Eiffel Tower, and she ran right into my arms. I might have cried a little behind my sunglasses. I was over-whelmed at the effect my presence had on her, and also with the swell-ing of my heart. I was never not going to show up for this girl.

So, I kept showing up. I went to Whoopsie's soccer game each week, and when Oopsie signed up for surfing classes, I went to watch her in the water.

By this point, I was about five months into therapy with Dan. He gave me a book called *Brainstorm,* which he had written about child brain development. I figured peppering in a little child psychology would be a worthwhile addition to my course load.

I learned about the four S's: seen, safe, secure, and soothed. These are what Dan says are the most important things for a child to feel. So, that became my edict. *Seen, safe, secure, soothed.*

I was going to provide comfort and healing to these girls. I spent many afternoons with the two youngest ones at Yogurtland or a Star-bucks, or we'd get my dogs and let them run freely on the Santa Mon-ica beach, where dogs aren't allowed. The girls loved Bert and Bernice, and they'd ask to sleep at my house so they could be closer to them, but I didn't know what was appropriate and what wasn't. I was now only communicating with their mother, who was and has always been very supportive of my relationship with all three girls. I wasn't sure what my ex thought of the whole arrangement, because his job prevented him from being at any games, practices, or recitals and he and I still hadn't spoken since the breakup.

Whoopsie, in particular, was having a difficult time. She was acting out a lot, doing dramatic things to get attention, constantly fighting with her classmates, and very obstinate with both her mother and her father. I somehow became the de facto mediator in the family, and whenever Whoopsie got into trouble at school, her mother would text me to let me know. I continued working with Whoopsie on her schoolwork, on her attitude, and just showering her with love and support. She was the most similar to me, and I felt her pain. I knew how unpleasant adolescent girls could be to each other, how massively important it all feels at the time—and how little impact it actually has on the rest of your life.

Then, one Saturday night at two in the morning, I got a phone call from Poopsie, who had just been pulled over by the police for a sobriety check. This was the first time I had heard from her since the breakup. She had passed the sobriety check, but she was so freaked-out she drove to the first parking lot she saw and parked her car. I went and picked her up in the middle of the night and brought her home to my house. She slept in my bed that night, holding my hand. In the morning, we stopped and grabbed a bagel for breakfast, and then I dropped her off where she had left her car. She and I never spoke about it, and I decided telling her parents wasn't necessary, since nothing had actually happened and my loyalties at this point were to the children and making them feel safe.

It was hard to really grasp what I had gotten myself into with this dysfunction junction of a family, but I also knew that every family is dysfunctional, and that I had a role here, even though I had no idea what that role was called. I wasn't their sister, mother, or father—or even stepfather. I was an outsider who got nestled into the role of family counselor. It was absurd, but the love and affection I had developed for all three girls overrode any sort of appropriateness.

De Facto Parenting

Five years after we first met, Whoopsie and Oopsie were still in my life. Poopsie had gone off to college, and I would hear from her occasionally, but she was living her new life. I was traveling again, performing, and I wasn't around as much as I had been when I first met the girls.

Whenever I was in L.A., I went to their school plays and soccer games and took them out for dinner—all the while getting sideways glances from the other parents at their school, who were wondering what the hell I was doing hanging around with other people's children.

By this point, their dad and I were on better terms, and we had an open dialogue about the girls and the time I was spending with them. He thanked me for the difference I had made in their lives. He said that it made him want to be a better father, and that my time with their family had shown him what it meant to be present, consistent, and available, that his relationship with the girls had improved drastically—and also, was there any way I could take the two girls away for part of their summer? He and his ex would both be traveling for the month of July, and Poopsie had gotten herself a summer internship, so the two young girls were on their own.

A few of my friends said that I was allowing myself to be manipulated by both my ex and his ex-wife. They said I had become a nanny, and I was being completely taken advantage of. Some of my friends questioned my level of involvement in these kids' lives and suggested that problems would arise—not only with my ex-boyfriend, but with any future girlfriends he might have, with their mom, and with the girls themselves. I didn't give a shit. I didn't care if I was being manipulated by the parents. I loved these girls, and I wasn't going to let the worry of potential future problems interrupt what joyfulness we were all experiencing in the present.

The girls and I had bonded, and there was no going back. I wasn't going to abandon them, ever. Especially when I had the means to bring them with me whenever I could.

So, that summer, I took the younger girls with me on my summer vacation to Mallorca. At the height of their adolescent angst, I wanted them to see how big and beautiful this world is. How small TikTok is, how silly middle school cliques are, and that peace and harmony exist on a planet that can seem terribly cruel.

To say this was a challenging trip would be an understatement because the girls had been through a lot, and there was a lot of fighting, a lot of tension, and a lot of bad habits of communication. Jealousy, trauma, neglect, all of it came crashing down, and it made for a lot of emotional highs and lows. One of my nieces, who was also on the trip, told me that thinking I could heal them by taking them to Mallorca was a mistake. I didn't think that Mallorca would be a magic wand. I thought that it would be healing to take them, and that oftentimes healing doesn't happen in the moment. It can happen in many moments, and long after the trip itself more healing can take place. To me, this trip was part of a process, an example of letting them know that there is another person in their lives who is going to be consistent with their love, consistent with their care, and someone who will keep showing up.

The girls were now thirteen and fourteen. Their hormones were in full swing, and it was a lot different from snuggling with an eight-year-old. They fought with each other constantly, and when they weren't fighting with each other, they were fighting about who was getting more attention. It was pretty exhausting to always feel like I couldn't do anything right. The three of us had grown so close it was like we were our own little family.

So, when we returned from Mallorca, like any responsible stepparent, I took it upon myself to reach out to a family psychologist who specializes in parental coaching, and I started taking weekly parenting classes. Yes, you read that right. The person who is pilloried for being "anti-children" was now taking weekly parenting classes and I was learning a ton.

I learned about parentification, which is when the parent has placed too much responsibility on the child, who in turn becomes dominant because they are now involved in their own parenting, which leads them to believe their parent is not capable on their own. This dominant behavior in adolescents especially is a result of feeling unsafe and not secure in their own home and family dynamic. Essentially, the child is scared, and in turn they become dominant as a defense mechanism. The response to this is to show up consistently, provide safety and security through food, presence, positive reinforcement, and lots of love. Consistency is the key. I'd have to regularly show up, to always reinforce that I am available, and to check in with the girls all the time, especially when I went to Whistler for the winter. Since they have had so much separation in their lives, I learned that during any separation it is very important to constantly check in. To reassure them in my absence that I was still available. To keep distributing my love evenly and to not participate in any of the arguing going on between them or between them and their parents. To provide a safe haven. To love, love, love them up.

My part-time parenting needed to shift into full-time parenting, so I stepped up my game and made sure I became a constant presence instead of a seasonal one.

I took my parenting classes pretty seriously because I was learning so much about my own childhood rebellion, and about children and parents in general.

I started from a place of discipline and bribery and thought I could whip the girls into shape by leveraging all I had to offer. I learned that parenting is not bribery but unadulterated, uninterrupted love. To feed them with love and, when they are scared, to feed them with more love. To let them know I am not going anywhere. To be constant and to show up when things are good and when they are bad. To sit in silence when no one wants to talk, but to remain as a presence. To not meet them with anger when they are angry and act out. To meet them with love. To reward them for good behavior and to be there in the bad. To tell them they are beautiful inside and out, to talk about how valuable knowledge is, and encourage them to study and keep reading, and to make sure they each know that they are a priority in my life.

But also to make time for fun, to stay awake for board games I don't care about, to have patience for the trivialness that comes with teen angst. To let them do my hair and makeup, even though I'd rather not sit down to get my hair and makeup done. To watch videos of things I'll never remember. To remain interested in any interests they have. To understand that as long as someone can cry, their heart is still soft and loving, and there is vulnerability. To show them sacrifice. To show them how big the world is and how much of an impact you can have on others. And to never get angry. That you can't heal anyone with anger.

One night, I took Whoopsie and some of her friends to see Fortune Feimster's stand-up show in Los Angeles. We hung out backstage with Fortune after the show, and then we all headed back home.

"Father, do you want to listen to the playlist I play when I want to relax?" Whoopsie asked me, as we sat in the back seat holding hands on the drive home.

"Obviously," I told her, squeezing her hand.

She played music by this young artist named Waxahatchee, a world I hadn't known of hers. We sat listening to one song after another on her playlist, while she shared her own private world of music, the songs that soothe and inspire her. I wondered how many other secrets and private cup filler uppers she had in her life that I hadn't yet been introduced to. She was only fourteen now, but she had a whole world of her own, a whole life of her own, and I felt deep love in my heart for her individuality and her desire to share it with me.

I told her how beautiful her music was. That I was so happy to hear it and know that she had a playlist like this.

"Will you send me this playlist so that when I'm on the road, I can listen to it and think of you?" I asked her.

"Father, this is one of the memories I'm going to write down tonight; this is a core memory," she told me. When Whoopsie looks at me, it is with heaps of rainbows in her eyes, and it melts me every time. "I'll save it with Fortune's backstage pass. I've saved every plane ticket, every show pass, every picture, and I write down everything we've ever done together. Because you have given me so many memories, and you're the best father I've ever had."

So, when people tell me I'm irresponsible for spreading positive messages about remaining childless, I smile, knowing that I have been a parent to many, and knowing the biggest gift I have ever been given was becoming a father.

I want to be sitting on my deathbed
knowing that I went for it. I'm going to get
sick and die at some point, and I would
like in that moment to smile at the life I lived.
That I had Guts. That I had standards.
That I loved people intensely.
That I lived in a loud, brave way.

Wisdom 2.0

Winters in Whistler fly by, and the month of April, when I'm supposed to head back to L.A., always seems to sneak up on me. One early April, I was scheduled to be interviewed onstage at a mindfulness conference in San Francisco, called Wisdom 2.0. So I knew I would have to pack up the house and return to California.

Wisdom 2.0 is a conference that has lots of neuroscientists, lots of psychologists, and many proponents of the psychedelic and micro-dosing community who speak about the benefits and research they've discovered using LSD, psilocybin, and MDMA. Michael Pollan was interviewed onstage about his book *How to Change Your Mind.* A lot of interesting conversations happen at this conference, and my therapist Dan and I were asked to do a panel about our working relationship and my book that was born out of it.

While I am definitely someone who looks in the mirror a lot, I had somehow missed that during my winter in Whistler my face had changed into two completely different colors. The top part, which had been covered by ski goggles, remained its original color. But the bottom half of my face—the part that was exposed to sun and wind—was about eight shades darker.

When my makeup artist came to my hotel room to help get me ready for the conference, she studied my face with extreme consternation.

She turned my chair so that we both faced the mirror, and we looked at me. "Which way . . . do you want to go?" she asked. I was befuddled. How had I missed seeing my face had become two very different colors?

"I don't think we can go darker," I said. "That's getting into Rachel Dolezal territory."

I looked like a giant dick that day, but it wasn't the first time, and anyone reading this knows it won't be the last.

Just like my face, there is light and there is darkness, and they very consistently follow each other around, like partners.

Public Love

For the longest time, I likened therapy and meditation to using emojis: there were certain types of people who did those things, and I wasn't one of them. By the time I was in my mid-forties, I was using all three, daily.

My sister Simone replied to a text I sent her, asking, "What's up with the eggplant emoji? That's not for your sister."

I explained that I was trying to harmonize my spirituality with humor and implement it into every facet of my life.

"Uh-huh," she wrote, disinterested. I couldn't shut up about therapy, and my family was over it; they were sick of being dragged into whatever new trend or fad I had chosen to apply to my life.

"Don't worry. I'm done making public pronouncements about anything. I just want to live in harmony and meet everyone where they are."

"Except for publicly pronouncing how in love you are with Joe Koy," she reminded me.

I didn't have the energy to disagree, mostly because she wasn't wrong. I had spent my personal and professional life telling everyone what they were doing wrong—solicited or unsolicited—and screaming about how in love I was would have definitely garnered criticism from yours truly. But the truth was, I couldn't help myself. I couldn't help sharing with the world how the unimaginable had happened. How my heart had been blown open and I'd fallen head over heels with an actual man.

Like many impressionable young girls, I had spent years fantasizing about what my perfect guy would be like—and in all my hopes and dreams, someone with smaller thighs than mine had never entered the realm of my imagination.

I had devoted a great deal of my time during my thirties and forties to globe-trotting in search of adventure and experience and hoping that along the way I'd bump into the love of my life. It was unlikely he'd be American, I always knew; he'd have to be a foreigner. There would have to be some sort of language barrier for me and a man to see eye to eye.

I had spent about a year reconnecting and hanging out as friends with Joe Koy when I was smacked in the face one night with the realization that I was falling in love with him. I was sitting outside at some YouTuber's house when I noticed him in a conversation with a dozen people inside the kitchen. I saw that he was staring right through the window at me. Like a laser beam.

He went and got a red plastic cup, filled it with ice, walked outside, and asked, "Were you looking for ice?" Then he handed me my lip balm. I am *always* looking for more ice and I am always looking for my lip balm. These are the kinds of things that make me feel cared for—the small gestures that show me someone is paying attention. I don't need jewelry or lavish gifts, or big-ticket items from a guy. I can buy all those things for myself, which is part of the reason it is so hard to date. When men realize you don't need anything from them, they have trouble recognizing their own added value.

Since I have my own money, my own life, and a career that keeps me busy, I am really only accepting relationship candidates who are not a subtraction. I need someone who is going to add something I don't already have—like the love and consideration that a partner can bring. I need someone who is paying attention. Someone who understands my relationship with lip balm and ice. Someone who wants me to know that my comfort and happiness are a priority for him.

I wanted to lean into Joe Koy and hug him and tell him thank you for looking at me like that. I knew in that moment that he was in love with me. I guess I had always known, but like any girl hanging out with a guy she suspects has a crush on her, I figured we would just hang out until he crossed a line and the situation became unmanageable. I never thought I would fall in love with him, too. Old wounds, childish tendencies, having my guard up, and not really knowing true intimacy: these were all coats I was actively shedding post-therapy. But while we are shedding, there are moments when the old skin is still hanging on by a thread, and the new skin is very desperately trying to break through.

Not only did I feel the love, but I felt compelled to share it with anyone who would listen—because I finally had my love story. I was *finally* the girl getting the happy ending that everyone always talked about. I had found *and accepted* true, deep meaningful love, and it made me want it for every single person alive. I wanted everyone to know what this kind of love felt like. I wanted to shout it from the rooftops—so I started with our most modern-day rooftop: Instagram. Joe lit up anytime I spoke about him publicly, so I did it any chance I got. I wanted him to feel secure and loved and to know he could depend on me.

Before therapy, I hadn't realized how closed off I had been because of my brother dying. I knew I had intimacy issues, but I didn't put a lot of weight into them, because I believed that if and when the right person came along, he would fix me.

Now that my eyes were more open, there was a new sense of possibility. Things I would have dismissed or denounced earlier came into view without me rejecting them. The frequent shopping trips, the obsession with fancy sneakers, the steady rotations of showy sports cars, or even watching a UFC fight all became things I decided to have a good attitude about.

I had never been in this kind of relationship before—one where there was never a question of either person's interest in spending every free minute together. I loved that about him and us. I wanted to be with Joe all the time, and I never had to wonder if he felt the same. We'd go out to eat, and if I had a drink, he had a drink. If I smoked a joint, he smoked a joint. If I took a month off drinking, he took a month off drinking. I envied him for being so adaptable, and in turn I worked harder on my own adaptability.

With Joe, I felt like I was being loved by someone for the very first time, and it felt like so many different things at once. Sweet, comfortable, at times suffocating, but also like I had a partner, a best friend who would cook me ramen at night (instant) and rub my feet while we watched movies. It felt a lot like a mother's love.

Falling in love and seeing how much this guy cared for me made me feel like I was winning. I had been so lucky in my life with my family, my career, and my friendships. I had been given so much already. I had doubted for so long that I would ever get the love part, too, and I had accepted that. When Joe came along, I felt like I had finally been gifted the thing that little girls dream about: someone who really sees you. Someone I didn't have to shrink myself for, or worry about emasculating. I had finally found my person, and this meant the universe had my back.

I had never dated a comedian before, because male comedians can be moody, dark, and sometimes quite depressed. Joe is none of those things. He is not selfish. He is giving and he is loving, and he is generous with his affection and attention. When he loves you, it feels like the entire sun is shining down on you. He's also a gentleman. He would never let me open a car door, carry my own bag or even my purse. Knowing my addiction to Vaseline lip balm and need to apply it every thirty minutes, he would carry an extra tube of it in his pocket and leave one in his car. Whenever I started looking for my lip balm, he'd pull his out and hand it to me. If I were to discuss this with someone who practices medicine, they would deduce pretty quickly that I am in a constant state of dehydration, but I am only realizing it now as I type this sentence.

We were both on tour and I was in Kansas City, Missouri, for two nights and he was performing in St. Louis for two nights. My crew and I were upstairs eating dinner after my show in my suite when he knocked on the door to surprise me. He had driven four hours to sleep in the same bed with me and would have to drive the four hours back in the morning for his show the following night. It was such a sweet gesture and I remember flying out of my seat and jumping into his arms. I would like to go on the record and say, I would never drive four hours to sleep with anyone.

It felt like Joe had waited patiently for me, and when the time was right, he kept showing up. This would be the man I would spend the rest of my life with. We fit. He was my guy, and I was done with any other men.

I was bending, compromising, and meeting Joe in the middle on all sorts of things, something I hadn't been willing to do in any previous relationships. My opinions had always been fully formed and not negotiable. Nothing about me before therapy was compromising.

As someone from New Jersey who grew up in shopping malls, my preference had been to never set foot in a shopping mall again. I avoid them like I avoid adult Halloween parties. Now here I was, going to actual shopping malls, getting my ears pierced at said shopping malls, and having fun while doing it. It felt good to not be so rigid, to loosen up a bit. I hadn't realized how tightly wound I had been.

We were once sitting in my backyard and Joe noticed a blue jay and asked me what I thought the bird was thinking. He had this sweetness, this innocence about him; he was able to look at all living things and see them. I'm not like that. When I see a bird, I'm not thinking about what that bird is thinking about. I'm thinking about how well rounded I am that I'm paying attention to birds. I may even wonder if that bird is stunned by my intelligence. Or in many instances, I'm thinking that the bird is my mother coming to say hello. The bird is always about me; it's never just a bird.

My sisters had noticed the difference in me. They commented on my newfound desire to prove that I was more than just my own needs and wants. I wanted to be a person who was able to put other people's needs first, and I wanted to open my heart in a trustful way. To flip all of my previous relationship conditions on their heads. With Joe, I was doing that and the relationship lit me up and let me fly. He renewed my faith in men and restored my confidence in myself. I am here for a reason, and I had forgotten what that reason was, and how powerful my voice could be.

I also loved the feeling of everyone being so happy for me. It felt like they were celebrating me for growing up and falling in love. I had never felt that before. Giving people hope and making them happy was exactly what I had been missing. I felt what it must be like to be a good girl, a straight-A student, the head cheerleader—and I was down with all the positivity. I had never been a people pleaser before, but I was beginning to understand how the act of people pleasing had even begun in the first place. It felt like I was contributing something. I had grown so accustomed to criticism in my public life, I had no idea there could be so much public support for my personal happiness. I wanted to make sure that I enjoyed every minute of being in love and to make sure that I was there for the guy I was dating in the same way he was there for me. Which meant every free moment and even many of our non-free moments were spent together. We were inseparable, and between being on tour and being newly in love, I was spending less and less time with my friends.

I remember a girlfriend of mine saying to me at dinner, "Don't let yourself get lost in him, Chelsea."

I looked at her and let out a laugh. "As if I would allow myself to get lost in someone." I meant it. That period of my life was over. *I'm not getting lost, honey. It's not even possible.*

Breaking Apart

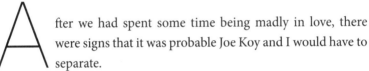fter we had spent some time being madly in love, there were signs that it was probable Joe Koy and I would have to separate.

When I saw the writing on the wall, we tried therapy together with Dan, but that only escalated things to a point where I knew our relationship needed a pause. We were a week away from taking twenty of our nieces and nephews on a two-week trip to Hawaii. The timing couldn't have been worse, and having to disappoint the kids made me sick to my stomach, but breakups are never timely, and making difficult decisions is part of being an adult. Appeasing other people in exchange for my own discomfort is something I am no longer willing to do.

If this were a tell-all, this would be the part where I would share every detail about what in fact happened in my relationship with Joe that turned it so drastically on its head. While I am sure that is of interest to people, I will no longer throw someone I once loved under a bus. My sharing what exactly went wrong in our relationship would negate all the work I have done on myself while also creating a headline I don't want to create. I have grown and learned, and I want to behave in a different way. I know that by choosing discretion when other people's feelings are at stake, I am a step closer to finding this woman I've been chasing around. All I will say is that Joe and I had different ideas about what being in a relationship meant. No one cheated. We were very much in love when we broke up, but after multiple conversations about what he expected a relationship to look like, I had to make a choice between him and myself. And I chose myself.

Ugh. The moment you know it can't work. The dreadful realization that you can't be in the relationship and truly remain who you are and who you've grown yourself to be.

This was the work of therapy: being in a relationship, being vulnerable without experiencing all the feelings that come with prior relationships when they go south—the desperation to make things right, the panic that you feel when something is ending, the rage toward the other person for not understanding that they are being unreasonable, or the very childish urge to prove you are right—I had none of these emotions. What I felt was sadness, and not the unbearable kind. The sadness of knowing that in order to make something work, I would have to abandon myself. The sadness of knowing there would be no compromise. That I am whole, that I am grounded, that I am full of love and gratitude, and even with all of these things, that the relationship was untenable.

I had spent two years unearthing all of my childhood trauma, and I assumed because of that I would attract the same. Instead, I attracted one of the greatest guys I have ever known, but he had never unearthed his trauma, and when the surface was scratched, it became clear that he had his own unfinished business, and that being so deeply in love with each other was triggering that trauma.

Then there was the public aspect of things. That was obviously something to consider, but it could never be my driving force in making decisions. Part of the reason I had been so publicly demonstrative about my feelings for Joe was that I knew he needed that. He wanted the validation, and I had no problem feeding it up. Especially when the public's response was so warm, and people were so inspired by our story. I loved having people run up to us on the streets of New York City, saying that we helped them to believe in love again—that if I could find love, then it was possible for them to find it, too. I believed that there was someone for everyone, and that as long as you never lower your standards, your person is coming. I still believe that and know that each person you love brings value that you didn't have before. That just because a relationship is over doesn't mean you have been defeated. Triumph isn't always winning. Triumph is being grounded enough to know that people will come and go in your life—and instead of racking up all the reasons they deserved to go by being bitter or angry, remembering the things they brought out in you that no one had before. How I conduct myself in every relationship whether people are watching or not is what true character is, and I had grown too self-assured to question whether I was making the right choice.

I thought back to my high school yearbook, where on my senior picture day I styled myself to look exactly like Jon Bon Jovi. Everyone had to choose a song lyric that they thought most aptly described them. I chose "It's better to have lost in love than never to have loved at all." I laughed out loud every time I saw my yearbook after that. As if a seventeen-year-old knows anything about losing out on love. Now here I was at age forty-seven thinking, *That's a pretty solid lyric.*

Girls Behaving Badly

have mishandled the endings of relationships before. I have conducted myself poorly within them and also while getting out of them, and I have many regrets when looking back at my behavior. I have been in unhealthy romances and I knew they were wrong, or past their expiration date, and I have ignored my good instincts. I have disregarded red flags and told myself stories about why I was the one at fault, or why I overreacted, or that I was paranoid. I no longer wanted to be a person who felt something and ignored it. I wanted to be a fully realized woman who had principles, and I wanted to be dignified in my actions.

My last relationship before therapy was a toxic one, with a man whom I was madly in love with, but whom I just didn't like very much. He would never be a friend, only a lover or ex-lover. One of the things I had promised myself was not to get into another serious romantic relationship until I could behave in a mature, trusting way and pick someone who could offer the same things back to me.

My pattern in that volatile relationship was to slam the door, not really mean it, and then very dramatically have my assistant ship all of my stuff out of my ex's apartment in New York City and back to my house in L.A. Then, three months later, one of us would call the other at 2:00 a.m.—we'd get back together and start the cycle again. Each time, I'd convince myself that enough time had elapsed for him to realize what he had lost in me, and because of that false notion I always believed he was ready to change his entire way of being. I dated someone on and off for almost two years whom I didn't trust, who lied and cheated, but whom I kept going back to by believing I could change him and the relationship. I blamed him for all of the toxic behavior, and then I blamed him for lowering my own standards.

This man and I had a great big love affair, and he swept me off my feet in many ways. We would work our way back and forth across the country to both cities, and then around the world to make incredible memories in cities across the globe. We laughed until we cried, and he was responsible for introducing me to so many things I hadn't seen before. He introduced me to cultures I knew nothing about, to poetry, to books written by philosophers I had never had the inclination to pursue. We'd spend one romantic weekend after another at one of his homes and slosh around in the mud on his farm, drinking champagne and taking pictures of each other chasing pigs in their sloughs, riding ATVs, and taking horse-drawn carriage rides through upstate New York. We even had our own stupid language we created that made us howl with laughter. It was a relationship worth having, but it went on for too long, and I didn't have the wherewithal at that time in my life to understand when things are so heightened, they are unsustainable. It's simple physics. What goes up must come down, and there is a place for calm in all of the storms, but if you are uncomfortable in that calm or without the storm, then you cannot survive and there will be a break in the foundation—because there most likely never was a foundation. I learned so much about myself in that relationship, but not while I was in it—only after it ended.

This seems to be the way many of us do things. We jump into a job, or a friendship, or a romantic relationship, and we flail around trying to keep our head above water sensing that things aren't necessarily right, but ignoring that knowing feeling, and instead we just struggle to stay afloat. This was starting to become a pattern with me: ignoring my inner voice, and believing my personality was strong enough to make something into what I wanted it to be. I didn't know yet that not everyone in your life is supposed to be there forever.

After my time with Dan, I understood that no one makes you lower your own standards but yourself. I didn't want to be in a relationship again where I mistrusted someone, or spent my time going through someone's phone. I didn't like that version of myself and I would no longer behave in such an insecure way, or not take at face value what someone said. I had devalued myself in that relationship.

Somewhere along the way, I lost my footing, and I needed to get back on track. I wasn't going to reduce myself once more to screaming and yelling, throwing tantrums about how someone disrespected me, or threatening to never see a person again. Words lose their meaning when they are repeated too many times, empty threats are vapid, and it is childish to think that you can change someone by cutting them off. What I know now is that you don't get respect by demanding it. You get it by giving it. *This isn't the woman that you always dreamed of becoming. She would never act this way.*

I wanted to be soft, instead of terminal. Acting in anger and haste had only led me to spit out vitriol, rather than thoughtfulness, and yes, certain relationships are toxic and deserve to end, but there is no reason to do that with anger or vindictiveness. Sometimes, you just need to let go. It doesn't have to be a war.

Healing Through

S o, here I was, many years post-therapy, hundreds of hours of meditation under my belt, with a softer, more loving and open-minded version of myself. I knew what lay before me was a huge opportunity for growth.

It had taken me decades to learn how to not lay blame, to not be punitive or vindictive when someone hurts me. To be mindful and consistent while recognizing the difference between instinct and impulse. To recognize that instinct is a knowing feeling, and impulse is acting on an emotion. I made sure not to go out of my way to see things or to spy on my ex on social media or any of the nonsense that can go along with heartbreak these days, which helped in making the distance between us grow greater, and helped erode the familiarity of having him around. It also helped me feel mature.

If we were ever going to get back together, I knew that space and time were necessary, and if we didn't get back together, then space and time would also be necessary to assess what my part was—and to perhaps accept that this love was only part of my story, rather than *the* story. Joe had been a catalyst for the opening of my heart and mind, and my job after we broke up was to keep them both open. He had helped lead me to a better place, and even though he and I were separating from each other, I still had every right to remain standing in this new better place. *I am not here because of you; I am here by way of you,* I kept reminding myself.

The very meaning of a full existence on this earth is to find out who you are and why you are here. Universal intelligence is the idea that when things don't turn out your way, it is because the universe is protecting you and steering you in a different direction. We all need to spend less time questioning disappointments or rejections. This is hard. It is a practice, and it is a test you will keep encountering until you ace it. The spiritual medium Laura Lynne Jackson, who has become a close friend and sounding board during some of my darker times, describes this as a soul test. She says that when you ace a soul test, your soul is elevated. This is a graduation of sorts. Getting on your highest soul path doesn't mean that the tests end. They keep coming, and you have the choice to keep getting better at mastering these tests. It can be losing a job that you thought was yours, or a romantic relationship that was yours, or a friendship that you thought was yours.

My breakup with Joe was a test for me to reach a higher path, one where I didn't reduce myself to match the way I felt. *Here is an opportunity for growth, for soul elevation. If you handle this with grace, you will graduate from that old self.*

I had been taught to look at my emotions with my brain, and not the other way around—to not let my emotions run me, to let my good sense of self drive me. My only goal was to stay elevated. There was no reason for any communication that was harsh or mean or dismissive. I held on to all the love I had in my heart and tried to push it out around me and envelop myself in it.

To know that the only thing to do when you are in deep pain is to give out love to any friend or stranger who is in need, so that's what I did. I expanded my love, my generosity, my virtue, my patience, and my soul. *Open, open, open. Love out.*

This became a perfect opportunity for me to practice my gratitude. To remind myself that even in the midst of heartbreak there was still so much to be grateful for.

> July 11: Am grateful for my experience in this relationship and am grateful for everything I am feeling. Heartache, disappointment, frustration, but happy inside for all that it showed me about being in love. I'd like to do that again.

> July 12: Finding gratitude today for Bert and Bernice and how much joy they bring me, just by looking at their bodies.

> July 13: Grateful to all the people checking in on me.

> July 14: Grateful for the mental clarity this time away from Joe Koy has brought me. You're going to be just fine. Like you always are.

> July 16: Feeling pretty sad and like maybe I'm not cut out for romantic relationships. Maybe I don't have what it takes. Feeling sorry for myself.

> July 17: Feeling better today. Grateful for my strength of mind, and for books.

> July 18: Rereading *Circe* by Madeline Miller. First book I've ever read twice. Love the end of her chapters. Great sentence structure and punch with her writing. Very powerful. Grateful my dad made me read so much.

> July 19: I laughed a lot today. Felt so good to be laughing. I don't think I laughed for the last five days. Is that possible?

July 20: Bad day today. Mabel came home and found me crying on the couch. I told her I know how much she loved Joe Koy, and she said, "Of course, we love anyone you love, but you are our girl. You're the one we love the most."

Made me cry harder. I wonder if she thinks I am her actual baby.

July 21: This morning, I tripped over Bert and almost impaled myself on the stairway railing, and then caught the top of the railing to avoid falling down the entire staircase, and ended up hanging from it like I was hanging from a tall building. Bert didn't even wake up. So, things are getting back to normal. Sometimes, I feel like his head is made out of a block of cheddar.

The more I sat with myself, the more I meditated, the more I let myself feel without distraction or deflection, the closer I got to feeling my mother and my brother guiding me in a new direction. They were with me, and they were telling me everything was going to be okay, and this was the first time in my adult life that I felt confident that I was going to be okay and that I was going to survive.

Let it run out, and then you will be able to see how you really feel, I kept telling myself whenever I was overcome with emotion. I had to remember that when you are in the thick of grief, you can't see it clearly.

The morning after Joe and I broke up was a Sunday, and I was sitting in the living room of my rental house staring at the books on my coffee table. I cried and cried and I didn't turn on the TV, or go for a walk, or call any friends. I wanted to try the very thing I had read about, which was to sit in my pain without looking for someone to make me feel better. To let the grief work its way through and out of my body. This breakup wasn't going to break me. It was going to strengthen my resolve to be the best and most evolved version of myself that I could find. I wanted to *welcome the pain.*

But I was scheduled to guest host *Jimmy Kimmel Live!* for the entire week, beginning the next day. It was a blessing to be distracted by work and to spend my time developing monologues with the writers. *Roe v. Wade* had just been overturned and that became the perfect outlet for my anger and disappointment.

I knew I was putting my pain on pause for that week and that I was headed in the direction of some deep hurting—that my heart was going to break even more, and I had to accept that I was going to be in agony. Fear of these feelings is what keeps us stuck, what convinces us to stay in a broken relationship and keep trying. The fear of the anguish and the fear of the aloneness.

My broken heart was sending all sorts of signals to my consciousness. To feel pain, and be able to hold not only that pain but also joy for a friend's achievements or accomplishments, or what can sound unfathomable in the midst of grief: to be joyful for another when they have found what you just lost. Being able to do that is a sign that you are growing.

I have lots of friends who I've noticed are great at giving other people advice about their lives, but they're unable to apply that same sagelike clarity to their own lives. I wanted to become a person who was good at both, who would never treat myself with less care than I would anyone else who needed help.

I never believed I would get to have the kind of love affair that Joe and I had. I got a taste of what that can be, and because of that I knew then that it was possible and probable to happen again. I was grateful for my ability to receive love—and for finding gratitude in the dark.

I wasn't going to negate any of my graceful behavior with actions that would only set me back and fog up my vision of what time and space really mean. I wouldn't confuse missing someone with belonging with someone.

I became for myself what I've tried to be for every important person in my life, my own best friend. My own cheerleader, my own listener, my mother, my sister, I became my own daughter.

My goal was to get over my heartbreak from losing my relationship without shutting the door on Joe permanently. I have a long history of shutting doors, and I wanted to break old patterns and create new ones. As I've grown up and out, I've learned this was a maladaptive strategy I had picked up from a very young age, which is quite the opposite of healing and growth. I know now that slammed doors are usually shut forever; it was important to me to throw my foot in the door of our relationship to try to keep the smallest opening—not for the hopes of getting back together, but for an exercise in maturity and compassion. Compassion for what the other person might be going through, understanding that my life experience was not his, and because there was no real way for me to understand how he saw things.

I had to continually remind myself that I was not the only person going through something difficult, or the only person going through a breakup with someone they still loved, and to remember in your darkest hours that there are much more serious predicaments to be in, and that a breakup isn't cancer, or death, or the end of the world. It's a breakup, and you will survive.

> July 30: Did Glennon and Abby's podcast, *We Can Do Hard Things*. I had already rescheduled twice, and our breakup became public yesterday, so I leaned in, and was vulnerable and honest, without telling anyone exactly what happened. I woke up this morning to sixteen thousand DMs from women thanking me for my honesty and vulnerability. I healed a bit of myself yesterday, and now all these random people I've never met are healing me more with their messages to me about bravery, vulnerabil-

ity, and honesty. It was the rainbow I had been looking for. Gratitude.

I had become so many of the things I had dreamed of becoming, and now I had my chance to show my younger self that I was everything I had imagined and more. *I've got you,* I told myself. *I'm right here, where I've always been.*

Self-examination is the key to growth
and self-expansion, but self-immolation
is the key to shrinking and setbacks.
Positivity and optimism can sound hollow
in certain situations, but when you instill
positivity and optimism into every situation,
miracles can and do happen.

Desperate Times

The idea that my confidence makes certain men feel insecure is pretty disheartening. Isn't it ideal for every little girl to grow up with confidence and for her to bloom? Shouldn't that be a delightful quality rather than one that yields disdain and comments like "she's too loud," or "too opinionated," or "too full of herself."

A couple months after my breakup, my friend Jen wanted to set me up on a date with a friend of hers who lived in New York City.

The guy and I had a decent date, went to dinner and then for some drinks afterward, but he seemed judgmental about the fact that I smoked a joint after our dinner, and also made a comment about my "lifestyle."

We were walking around SoHo when I stepped into the street and he came over and steered me back onto the sidewalk. Some people may think that is a sweet gesture, but I just find a man who tries to direct my actions, whether physical or emotional, to be someone who doesn't understand the type of woman I am.

"He seems like a dad," I told Jen after the date. "Which would be fine if he was one, but seeming like a dad without kids is not hot. It all just seemed so middle-aged."

"You *are* middle-aged," she reminded me. "That's what's out there."

"No," I told her. "That's not the only thing that's out there. If that's what's out there, I'd rather be alone. I'm not desperate."

The word "desperate" has no place in my vocabulary or life. There is nothing desperate about knowing your truth, your value, and not sublimating any of it for another person.

I'm not saying that it's better to be single than to be in a relationship, but I am saying that I am very happy in my own company, and I am not desperate to change that in any way. There are too many people in this world whose only prerequisite in liking a man or woman is that that man or woman likes them back. That's not enough of a reason to be with someone, ever.

Of course, there is joy in having a romantic partner and a family, and of course there are endless benefits to the levels of togetherness that those people and dynamics can bring. What I also know to be true is that there are myriad experiences that can bring these feelings to the surface as well. Self-love and self-determination are not aspects to be undervalued in terms of cultivating joyfulness. The way we love ourselves is a direct reflection of how we love others and how much we are willing to give. I know that when I take the time to fill my own cup rather than deplete it, the more bandwidth I have to give out. My aim is to be a high beam of love and generosity, a magnet for positivity, and a strong shoulder to lean on. And while I don't think this is every person's purpose, I do know that what I can contribute to the world is more profound and meaningful when I am full of the deep love I am capable of having for myself.

"Okay," Jen told me. "But, with that attitude, you're going to die alone."

I would like to go on record and say this is one of the most ridiculous sentences I've ever heard, and I hear it way too often. First of all, I very much want to die alone. The reason to have a partner or children should not be so that they will be there to watch you die. I look forward to paying some nurse or drug dealer to either put me down like a horse or help usher me out of this world with a large dose of morphine. I don't want anyone to watch me die or to be there with me. I just want to go to sleep and drift into whatever is next, and if there is absolutely nothing beyond this world, that's fine, too. I'm not that worried about it.

I have been practicing rather diligently to not be attached to the outcome of anything in life, and I am definitely not attached to the outcome of death. It seems preposterous to me to get married or to procreate in order to have someone by my side when I die. I can rent a person to do that.

Furthermore, the amount of time I have spent listening to women complain about losing complete autonomy over their lives due to having children would equal the amount of time it would take for me to complete a full-term pregnancy.

We don't give enough credit to all the childless heroes out there. We are not celebrated enough, and we should be: for owning our truth, and being responsible enough to know that some of us are not cut out for parenting.

When I get all that hate for talking about how awesome it is to be child-free, my self-respect deepens for knowing not to listen to what people wanted or expected from me—and for knowing I am someone who is incapable of being pushed around or bullied.

The implication of all that backlash is that if I don't want to have children, I am some sort of degenerate whose sexual exploits and drug use render me useless to society. I've written six *New York Times* bestsellers and hosted television shows for ten years of my life, among everything else I have done professionally, and the idea that you can't have fun while remaining professional is laughable. To me, being professional *is* being fun.

The shrill cries from grown middle-aged white men about my choosing not to procreate should be a gift to men. After all, I'm saving all men from another incarnation of me. No daughter of mine would behave in a way that wouldn't piss off the entire male species. And believe me, I would have a daughter. One who would most likely walk through the world with her top off, drinking whiskey and Cokes and driving a Vespa by the age of eight. The amount of pleasure that would bring me almost makes having a kid seem worthwhile, but then again, children aren't meant to be born for us to live out our fantasies. They are far more important than any of our unrealized dreams.

Act first and think later is exactly what many men do, with little consideration of the results of that behavior. Telling a woman who doesn't want children that she is being irresponsible by not procreating is as hypocritical as one can get. I'm proud of myself for knowing what I'm capable of. I'm proud that I haven't spent my life listening to men who think they know what's best for me.

I had three men in my life tell me buying my house in Mallorca would be a big economic mistake. I knew if three men in a row told me not to do something, it was imperative that I do the opposite. My house in Mallorca has provided hundreds of people with life-changing vacations. My house in Mallorca has provided me with some of my best adult memories, favorite sunsets, most meaningful conversations, and endless nights kayaking under the moon and the stars. I paid cash for that house as a gift to myself after *Chelsea Lately* ended, and I've written two books in that house. That house has paid dividends to me that are immeasurable. It has absolutely been one of the best decisions I've ever made in terms of adding to my happiness and the happiness I am able to bring others. And, it was a great economic investment.

The expansion of your belief system, values, opinions, exposure to different people and places are the seeds to us growing up and out. Having a narrow-minded view of things and going through life without your opinions being challenged will only help you remain the same. Some people aren't interested in expanding their thoughts, experiences, outlooks. But if you are looking for moments of unadulterated bliss, the quickest way to get there is to get out of your own way. Your own ego, your own mindset, and your rigidity can lead to harsh judgment of others and a strong dose of bitterness when observing people who are seeking enlightenment, spirituality, and growth.

This is the most important love story we have: the one with ourselves. The admonishment and disdain that come in response to a woman's relationship with herself are a great reflection of how slow and unchanging our society really is. With regard to race, feminism, the LGBTQ+ community, immigrants, poor people, education, there is an unwritten understanding among the world's most powerful men that all of these groups will be better off and perform more dutifully with a foot on their neck.

Don't spend your time alone being bitter about losing out on love, or unrequited love, or whatever you thought was going to happen that didn't. Use that time to get to know yourself. To be with yourself and read and travel and spend time with your family, friends, and anyone whom you love and who loves you. This time we get with ourselves is when some of our most seminal growth occurs. In these moments, instead of spending our energy resisting the reality of the situation, we can *accept* the situation; we can remember that there is a bigger love story waiting for all of us if we pay close enough attention. You loving yourself. That is *the* story. *You* are the love of your life.

Travelogues

decided to give myself a summer sabbatical because I had been on tour for three months, and after twenty-five years of doing stand-up, I finally understand that when I tour, I give the most of myself. I've learned how important my mental clarity is when doing my job. When I've done three months on tour, I need one, or two, or in this case three months off to let my freak flag fly. That means doing anything my great big heart and brain desire.

So after three months of the Little Big Bitch tour, I took some time to relax. My first stop was London. My first night there, I met a man at a dinner party. He was tall, British, with an adorable head of curly dark hair, and so, so handsome. I had known him casually for years, and I casually knew his wife as well.

"My wife thinks I'm an alcoholic," he told me, while we sat waiting for our second course. "She threw me out of the house."

I thought back to my very first book tour in London when I was twenty-seven years old and my publishers took me to a celebratory lunch at the Wolseley. We polished off three bottles of champagne between five of us, and then they all went right back to the office, while I had to go back to my hotel and crash. *Is this how people operate in London? I could get used to this,* I thought.

"Aren't all British people alcoholics?" I asked him.

"Pretty much," he assured me. "Except my wife. She doesn't drink much and thinks it keeps me out of the house."

"The drinking sounds like more of a symptom of whatever the real problem is, which is why you don't want to be in the house?"

I told him the story about going to my first British wedding years ago in the British countryside at some gorgeous manor that the bride's parents owned. It was one of those perfect British summer nights and the rehearsal dinner was held in their garden, which was a rather formal event. It all had a very *Great Gatsby* vibe to it. At around 11:00 p.m., the groom came streaking through the backyard buck naked and ran directly into a concrete wall, hitting his head hard and then ricocheting off the wall and onto the ground. It was obvious to me that the wedding would most certainly be called off, and that the groom would be carted off to some rehab center deep in the Cotswolds.

But the next day, no one said a word about the incident. It was entirely overlooked in a characteristically British way and the wedding went off without a hitch. During his toasts, the bride's father talked about how pleased he was that his daughter had found someone with such integrity and charm. I remember looking around at the other guests and at the date I was with, thinking, *Really?* This was the beginning of my introduction to English culture and the thought crossed my mind, *Maybe I should move to London.*

If something like that happened in Los Angeles, the groom would have been sent the very next morning to the Betty Ford Center. Everyone in America, and especially in Los Angeles, spends way too much time judging other people's drunken behavior. It's one thing if you're an asshole when you are drunk—like I was at Jane Fonda's—but it's another thing if someone just likes to have a good time and you find yourself in conversation about how "puffy they've gotten," or hear comments about "the drinking is catching up to her." It's quite sickening after a while to pay so much attention to other people's drinking,

especially when it has very little impact on your own life. Leave people alone, unless you have found them more than once passed out on
your bathroom floor.

The truth of the matter is, most people have a little problem with
one thing or another, and most people seem to be able to manage it
just fine.

"Anyway," he told me. "I guess I'm single now."

Perfect, I thought. I had just told my new female therapist that what
I really was interested in right now was having multiple different love
affairs with men all over the world, and some repeat customers. No
dishonesty, just vibrancy, aliveness, and a port in every storm. I want
someone in Mallorca, someone in New York, London, L.A. (which
was proving to be nearly impossible), and Whistler. "I want to be having more sex and with different people," I said right before embarking
on a three-month vacation across the globe.

"Well," she said. "Then let's make that happen for you." We had
spoken about building sexual tension instead of heading straight to
the bedroom with men, because what I learned from my relationship
with Joe Koy was that it was fun to build a flirtation—in fact, that's
pretty much the most exciting part. The texting, the flirting, the wondering when someone is going to make a move. I had been making
moves on all my sexual partners of late, and it was becoming boring.
I wanted to be pursued, not be the pursuer.

Bringing men home without any buildup felt more like a conquest
than a connection; I wanted to behave less like a man and more like a
woman.

As I sat next to this man at dinner, I thought to myself, *Well, it
seems like I found my London lover.* I was due to spend the next two
weeks in London going to Wimbledon, among other things, and the
timing couldn't have been more perfect for *A British Dalliance.*

We spent the next week going to parties, pubs, and the theater and
taking rain-soaked walks in the park, until one day the rain turned
into a lightning storm, and everyone knows the safest place to go dur-

ing a lightning storm is a bar. I didn't care that this guy drank a lot, because his personality never really changed that much and I also like to drink. I was keeping my summer open for whichever way the wind blew, and after three more dinners together that didn't end in sex, it was blowing toward him. After a week of heavy flirting, he grabbed me under a doorway to a restaurant and declared he was going to kiss me on the mouth. I had declared what I was looking for, and then it had landed right on my proverbial doorstep.

He was fun, very caring, a great listener, and very bright. We had read tons of the same books, teased each other a lot, and laughed riotously every time we were together. He said he was separated from his wife, which I thought meant he was in no position to become emotionally attached. *Even better,* I thought, *this will be the exact kind of little dalliance I've been looking for.* After my two weeks in London were up, he asked me to extend my trip for another two weeks, which I did. He was also living out of a hotel, so we were having a lot of fun bouncing between our hotels.

Then, one Sunday, we were supposed to meet for an afternoon drink and I got a text telling me that he was dealing with a very angry *spouse* who was preventing him from seeing his two sons, ages two and four. He said he hadn't been able to see them all weekend, and that he and his wife had a pretty ugly counseling session with their therapist. Would I be willing to wait to meet up until later that night after he figured out a way to see his kids?

I didn't respond.

I hadn't given much thought to his current situation because when he told me he was out of his house, I took that at face value and heard what I wanted to hear. Now I was realizing it wasn't that simple. He had said he got kicked out of his house, but I had ignored the fact that he wasn't even really separated. Now there was an angry woman—"spouse" was the word he used—involved. Not to mention two children. I sat on my bed and thought about what I was doing. You don't go to counseling with someone unless there is hope on one side or the other that the relationship can be rectified. This wasn't a man who was divorced—he wasn't even legally separated—and I was running around town with him like we were boyfriend and girlfriend. *Yikes,* I thought. *What have I gotten myself into?*

He texted me a few more times that night and tried to call me but I didn't answer. I needed to think about the repercussions of what I was doing. I talked to my girlfriend on the phone and she said, "Who cares? He's separated, you're only there for a few weeks, go have fun and then leave."

"Yeah," I told her. "Maybe. We'll see."

That didn't feel right. I had had an affair with a married man once when I was younger, and he had left his wife for me. I was in my twenties when that happened, and now I was in my forties. I knew better now. I wasn't going to be the cause of any marital disruption at this age. I had just extended my trip for two weeks to spend more time with this man, and I had a dozen reasons to justify continuing our little romance. Our crazy chemistry, our fun, my eventual departure: *Who cares?*

I stayed home that night and quite literally "slept on it" so that I could look at the situation in the morning with some clarity and less confusion. I woke up knowing that I wanted to put myself on a higher path, not a lower one. This was another test.

After his third text that morning trying to meet up with me, I finally responded.

Hi—
I am spending the day writing and have dinner plans tonight.
    I am going to put a pin in our little dalliance as your situation as exhibited this weekend is complicated and I really am just looking to have some fun without any drama.
    You're married—not even officially separated—and that isn't really the kind of woman I want to be.

You have a lot to deal with and I'd like to respect that.

As for hanging out together, I think that would also be a recipe for disaster considering the vibe between us and our chemistry.

As you well know, London can be a very small town and an escape for me from my real life. I don't want to be caught up in any drama.

I don't mean to sound harsh at all, but I have a way of living my life, and I need to honor that.

I know you'll understand.

X

My first instinct was to book a flight out of London the very next day to extricate myself from the situation. There is the moment when you draw a boundary, and the few days following that, the boundary can fade and you can easily get sucked back to where you were. I wanted to free myself from any temptation, but I thought what would be even more womanly would be to stay in London and resist any urge to see him. Next-level woman shit. So, that's what I did, and when he called or texted me, I didn't respond with anything other than kindness. Yes, I was very tempted to see him again, but the person I wanted to become wouldn't do that. She would stand by her word, and if he came around down the road at some point under a different set of circumstances, then she would reassess at that time. She wouldn't float that idea out to him—the woman I wanted to become wouldn't dangle the carrot of availability per his change of status. So I didn't.

People split up and divorce and cheat all the time, but we all have a choice to either be involved in someone else's marital demise or withdraw. My idea of me was stronger than my impulse, so I leveled up and became the idea I had of me: someone who respected other women, and someone who respected myself. I'm not a little girl who can't control herself, nor am I silly enough to believe that an attraction to someone is so overwhelming that there is no way out.

I finished what turned into a month in London, met a couple of different men who were nice distractions and a testament that there are *always* plenty of other options out there, and that when you make strong decisions, the universe rewards you. None of these guys and I had the same chemistry I had with the married guy, but that didn't matter. What mattered was that I had made a decision to remove myself from drama, from someone else's marriage, and in doing so, I'd told the universe that I was leveling up and would only consider men who were leveling up themselves. That decision led me to reunite with one of my favorite people in the world.

Sunny Side Up

don't like to use the word "literally," unless it's actually literal, so keep this in mind: it was literally the day after I said goodbye to the Englishman that I was sitting in a coffee shop working on my Spanish when I looked up and spotted Poopsie walking across the street.

Because of my obsession with grammar and verb conjugation, I was intent on making great strides in Spanish before I headed to Mallorca at the end of the month, and I was overloading myself with preparation, obsessing about the past, present, and future tenses of all irregular and regular verbs. I had come a long way from the very first sentence I learned, "Me gustaria un vodka con mucho hielo con un poco de soda." I'd like a vodka with a lot of ice and a splash of soda. My second sentence was, "Soy americana. Me gusta hielo." I'm American. I like ice.

"Poopsie," I yelled, running outside after her. "Poopsie, Whoopsie, Oopsie!!!" *Was it really her?* She stopped in her tracks and turned around.

"Father?" she screamed, seeing me jumping up and down. She ran back in my direction. She had a small dog in her arms and a large black shoulder bag swinging around like a wrecking ball. We collided, causing most of the contents of her bag to fall on the ground, which included several hairbrushes, dog treats, dog pee pads, and a pair of high heels.

That was Poopsie to a T. A beautiful mess who always had enough clothes in her purse to change from daytime to nighttime in an instant. We laughed at the pile on the sidewalk while we both leaned down to pick everything up.

I couldn't believe my eyes. I hadn't seen Poopsie in a few years, so I was delighted to see that not much had changed, while everything had changed. She was twenty-three now, living in London, and recently divorced. She was just as sweet and soft as she had always been, a beautiful girl, slightly heartbroken, listlessly bouncing around like a balloon in the sky.

We sat down at the café and she filled me in on everything happening in her life. She had moved to London straight out of college for a job and she had fallen in love with a British man. That relationship lasted two years, and now she was newly single, very scattered, and seemingly quite fragile. With Poopsie, it's easy to confuse her sweet nature with fragility, so in between all of our catching up and laughing, I was trying to assess what kind of shape she was really in. The only info I'd had about her for years came through her younger sisters. Poopsie and I talked and walked for hours that day, and then the next day, and the next day, and the day after that.

She revealed to me that when she left the States, it was because she didn't feel like her family was intact. She said that she and her sisters had grown up with so many inconsistencies. I understood her concerns well. She told me she appreciated that I didn't push her when she created distance between us, and that it hadn't been intended for me, but for her. She wanted to build her own family with her husband, and she thought they would be together forever, and now what?

· · ·

We spent the following two weeks strolling around London holding hands, eating delicious food, walking along the Thames, retelling the funniest stories about her sisters from that year we all spent together. We talked about that Valentine's Day we met. She said her relationship with her father had improved over the years. He had gotten remarried earlier that year to a woman who also had three daughters, so she had three new stepsisters.

"Perfect!" we exclaimed at the exact same time, clinking our Moscow mules together, laughing at the absurdity. We were sitting outside an art exhibit that we missed because we were an hour late arriving. Poopsie has never been early to anything in her life, and combined with my lack of navigational skills, we never arrived anywhere we were going in London until after the event was over.

When our server forgot to bring us a food menu and I got up to grab a couple for us, he came running over and apologized. "I'm so sorry," he told us. "I just got here by the skin of my teeth, and am already in the weeds. Please forgive me."

"Skin of his teeth?" Poopsie asked, after he left the table. "I don't understand that expression, Chels. Was something happening at some point where people had skin on their teeth?"

"That's a good question, Poopsie," I said. "I actually thought the expression was 'no skin off my back,' but I'm not clear on what that really means either."

"Well," she proclaimed. "There is definitely no skin on anyone's teeth."

"Except on yours," I corrected her, recalling a night in high school before she left for college where I was trying to impress upon her how important it was to brush and floss her teeth every day. Poopsie seemed to think brushing and flossing were optional.

"I hate flossing; it hurts, and my gums bleed," she would tell me at seventeen.

"That means you need to do it more. If you're bleeding when you floss, you are not flossing enough."

One night after dinner, while I demonstrated how to floss your teeth, I made her smell her own floss. My brother Glen once used this approach on me, and I hadn't stopped flossing since.

"I'm not smelling my floss," she said, years ago.

"Smell it," I said, shoving her face in it. When she recoiled from the smell of used dental floss, I knew I had cemented my argument.

"Do you understand now that those smells are living in your mouth until you remove them?"

"Yes, Father. I will never forget that smell," she told me.

"Chels, I still floss every day!" she exclaimed now, smiling, showing off her pearly whites and fabulous dental hygiene.

"I'm proud of you, Poopsie," I said "I'm proud of all of the things you have done, and for your big giant heart, and for your kindness to strangers and to the world."

"Really?" she asked me. "Are you proud that I'm only twenty-three and already divorced?"

"Yes! Be grateful it was only a year, honey. Half the people in the world get divorced after twenty years. At least you already got yours out of the way!"

We laughed, we cried, and I held on to her tightly as we made our way around town, talking about life, about picking yourself up, about not letting someone else define how you feel about yourself.

"I wish I had your confidence," she told me, while we were sitting in the park watching her dog run around on the grass.

"What's happening now is part of what is going to make you more confident. You have a choice here to rise up, and that's what we're going to do. We're going to pick you up, you and me together, and on the days you can't pick yourself up, I'll be there to carry you."

"Chels," she said, rearranging her sunglasses to sit on top of her head. "Did you just rip off 'Footprints in the Sand'?"

She was right. I had just unwittingly ripped off God, or whoever was in charge of writing that poem, and at the realization of this, we both went from tears of sadness to tears of laughter. My preferred turn of events.

One of my favorite scenes in a movie is in *Steel Magnolias,* when Sally Field's character is so angry after her daughter's funeral that she is screaming and crying and eventually says she just wants to "hit someone." Upon hearing this, Olympia Dukakis's character says, "Here, hit Ouiser! Hit Ouiser," and pushes Shirley MacLaine's character toward Sally Field, in order for her to hit her. It's the moment where anger and sadness collide into laughter, and the way it was captured in that film made me understand how life can be bearable when the worst happens, and that laughter is always the salve that comes— just when you think it is impossible to go on.

That's what happened to me and Poopsie that day in the park. We went from tears of sadness to tears of laughter, until we were both on the ground, holding on to each other, trying to catch our breath.

Poopsie looks like a princess and she is without guile. She has the kindest eyes and a face filled with warmth, and she needed to be reminded of how special she is and always will be. That she lights up rooms with her curiosity, her playfulness, and her sweet, sweet, good nature. Poopsie is a total lover. And she needed to get loved up.

I reminded her of what her dad used to say about her. That his favorite thing about her was that she woke up every day in a good mood; "Sunny Side Up" is what he used to call her. She doesn't have a mean bone in her body. She was always the softest, the most loving, and the most trusting.

I repeated this to her many times over the next two weeks, along with all the other things I wanted to imprint on her. That she is of value, with or without a husband, that getting married and divorced so young was going to turn into a blessing that she would most likely only be able to recognize later down the road. That she had her whole life ahead of her and now she had some time to refocus on herself, to figure out what she really wanted. That her ex was not the main character of her story. That she was and will always be the main character of her story, and that she is in charge of the ending to every chapter.

> July 10: Reunited with Poopsie! Took her to Wimbledon today and it was like no time had passed. She snuck her dog into Wimbledon inside her bag, and then he jumped out twice during Alcaraz match. Classic Poopsie. She recently got divorced, so her head is hanging a bit low. She'll be walking a little taller by the time I get done with her.

A couple of weeks later, it was time for me to meet up with all my nieces and nephews in Mallorca. I couldn't bear to say goodbye to Poopsie, so I thought it in both of our best interest for her to come with me to Mallorca. I wanted to inject her with some confidence, some like-minded female fierceness, and I wanted her to be surrounded by my nieces, who were close to her age. I knew my nieces would bring her in and wrap her up.

My three nieces are all quite different, but the one trait they all share is being secure about who they are, which is pretty much all I want for any young person. The three girls are talented in different ways, they read books, they don't care about social media, and not one of them gets led around. They are not followers. They have their own desires and tastes and they are true to who they are. I can see that they love themselves, and I knew in their hands Poopsie would thrive.

> July 30: Poopsie is getting loved up by my nieces and nephews and fits perfectly into our family. She is smiling and laughing all the time now, and thank goodness I had the good sense to free myself up from my London lover, because it provided me with the opportunity to do something way more important.

I had decreed that no parents were allowed on this vacation, but somehow my two brothers had infiltrated the trip under the subterfuge of "chaperones."

Apparently, it had been discussed within my family that I would have my hands full with so many children, and that I would need some assistance. No one in my family really understood that my life had become full of children—or thought me capable of managing young children in a foreign country—so along with eight nieces and nephews, Glen and Roy arrived.

Unfortunately, as a result of the Spanish speed HIIT classes I was taking, my Spanish accelerated beyond my understanding of the language. I could now speak in past and future tenses, but had lost my ability to communicate in the present tense, and it didn't take long before I stopped making sense in English. I turned to my brother Roy and asked him, "Can you please have gotten me a bite of that for us?"

"Come again?" Roy asked me, confused.

"Sorry about that," I told him. "I'm having a little trouble today with my Spanish and English sentence structure and pronunciation."

"Bon Iver, the Maldives, inexorable," Poopsie whispered to me. "Those are the three things I refuse to say out loud for fear of mispronunciation."

"I'm with you on Bon Iver," I told her. "I try not to say their name out loud as well."

"I had no idea you were so maternal," my brother Glen commented to me as we watched some of the kids run into the ocean moments later.

"I like to think of her as a nonbinary parental figure. It's not maternal or paternal," Poopsie said, as I applied sunblock to her back. "She's more than a sister, not quite a parent, but more reliable than most of the adults in my life."

"You're nonbinary?" Roy asked, turning toward me.

"I identify as a stepfather," I told him, as we followed the kids down to the beach.

"From matriarch to patriarch, Chelsea. You've had quite the arc," my brother Glen said.

I looked at my two brothers as I laid down a beach towel. "Well, with the two of you as the oldest men in our family, someone had to fill in as the patriarch."

"If we're being honest, I've always thought of you as my father," Roy added.

My family was together, and Poopsie was part of our family now, just like Oopsie and Whoopsie.

One of the great gifts my own family has given me is being so welcoming to all the people I've dragged into it. There have been a few rejections, but if I love someone deeply, my family welcomes them, too. They love them up and bring them in, because we all know how important it is to feel, to give, and to receive love. We are tight-knit, and we are dysfunctional, but we are kind and affectionate, and we always say "I love you" to each other. Because we know that to be loved is to give love, and all of our kids show this kindness, too.

"Come with me, Poopsie," my niece Charley said to her, grabbing her hand as they walked together down the beach. "I'm a Poopsie, too. We can Poopsie around together in the water."

> July 31: Poopsie left today, and she was walking taller, with her head a little higher and her spirit a little lighter. I love my Poopsies. Every single one of them.

My Man

t felt like my list of qualities I was looking for in a man needed an update. I wanted to make it very clear to whoever is in charge what I was expecting.

Please bring me someone strong, physically and mentally.

Someone who is emotionally available and insightful. Someone who has been to therapy.

Someone who doesn't scream or yell when they are angry. Someone who can talk about difficult emotions without being emotional.

Someone who cares about global politics and stays informed about the world.

Please bring me someone who brings out the best in me.

Please bring me someone who can teach me things.

Please bring me someone who is financially able to traipse around the world with me and who has the desire to do so.

Please bring me someone who understands me, loves me, and is not jealous of me being around other men.

Please bring me someone secure.

Please bring me someone whom I will come home to in the middle of the afternoon and find reading a book in our backyard.

Please bring me someone who respects women and shows compassion and grace to every group that has been underserved and marginalized.

Please give me someone who can laugh and get crazy, who can party, but keep their shit together. Someone who is as dependable as I am. Someone who is as on time as I am.

Please bring me my truest love yet.

I don't care where he's from or what he looks like. I want to love him for our chemistry and for his mind.

I want to be madly, deeply in love, in a healthy way.

There is no rush in finding this love. I am loving being single and untethered and laughing, and living. But I will remain open to the possibility when the right person comes along. I will remain ready for anything you serve me. I remain grateful for every person who comes into and out of my life. I am grateful for the joy as well as the pain.

Dependable, Kind, Munificent, Free

Dependable, kind, munificent, free. These are the words I want people to use when describing me. I want people to know how free I have felt in my life. How freedom can spread from one person to another and how valuable it is for other women to see someone taking their freedom and running with it.

I have always felt the strongest sense of freedom when I am leaving a job or a relationship that means something to me. To know that I am choosing myself always makes me recognize how powerful I am when I choose to be. Freedom isn't only knowing myself but trusting myself. To know that I have always been able to rely on myself. That I am strong, and that part of my strength is to know in moments of weakness that I will be strong again. To know that I will land on my feet. To trust myself. That is what freedom means to me.

It is something I have taken for granted many times in my life and I no longer do. Freedom to me is not being tethered to any one thing or person, but that is not to say I don't have responsibilities. I do, but only because I have placed them all there. I don't have to be generous, kind, or dependable, but those are my truths and my gifts in this life, and in recent years I've started to make very good use of them.

I'd been the opposite of those things in my early life, and I knew I wasn't living my real truth. I was out of balance, not thinking of others, searching, searching, searching for who I was supposed to become, and taking my freedom for granted.

Not every woman in this world has the luxury to ask herself, What is my purpose and whom and what do I deem as my responsibilities? There are women who will never feel the unadulterated bliss of skiing down a hill naked, making thousands of people laugh, or even what getting an education feels like. Freedom from slavery isn't something I can pretend to know about, no matter how many books I read or how many people I talk to. It is the same reason most men will have no idea what it feels like to be a woman.

I was born free and I was given a life that allowed me to reach for my stars, dream big, and then fearlessly go after those dreams. Being born white, middle-class, and cute was a great advantage in this life. I got a big head start in this world, and from early on I realized I would get what I wanted more quickly if I was willing to hustle. To constantly look around for opportunities, to stretch myself out of my comfort zone, and to make things happen, because no one was going to do that for me. People helped me along the way, but no one makes anything happen that you yourself aren't already working toward. To be laser focused on a goal and never taking it out of your peripheral vision means turning your dreams into a bowling ball that will knock over anything that gets in its way.

What freedom means to me is to be able to soar like an eagle when I want to fly, and to be able to wrap myself in bed for days in a row if that's what I need. Freedom is the sheer blissfulness I feel while riding my bike down the hills of Mallorca with no gears on, no pedaling, flying through the sky, with my very biggest smile on my face. The one that is pure ebullience and joy. I have dozens of smiles. I have smirks, flirtatious smiles, love smiles, happy smiles, polite ones, fake ones, and then the one where my eyes are bouncing off the moon—which is my biggest one.

My middle name is Joy, and I now understand that JOY is my purpose in life. To bring joy, comfort, understanding, DEPENDABILITY, to anyone who needs it. This joy that I want to spread and create doesn't come with any conditions. I am the wind blowing through a storm, the jolt of energy that I can bring to people who are in desperate need of a life boost.

I have never wanted children or to be married, and what that decision has freed me up to be for the rest of the world fills me with hope, love, and gratitude. I am here for women; that is my purpose. I am here to lift, to inspire, and to listen. There is not a woman in need that I wouldn't try to help pull out of whatever hole she is in to help lift her up. I am here for every member of the LGBTQ+ community and for any person who doesn't feel seen. I am here for the underdogs, and I am here to demonstrate compassion, empathy, and love. Once I identified my purpose, my bright bulb and effulgence began to shine. I am able to find joy in times of despair, and generosity in times of strife. My life has become even more than I could have imagined as a little girl sitting on my lawn waiting for the brother who never returned to explain himself to me.

I am here to remind every woman that each one of us is a queen, with or without a partner. To encourage women to respect themselves, to love themselves, and to stop looking around at what everyone else is doing. To pursue who we actually are, independent of the reflection of our jobs, husbands, wives, or families. You are valuable with or without a child, with or without what society tells us is valuable. We are significant all by ourselves, and my life experience thus far has shown me that the colors of my rainbow are bright, bold, and filled with ebullience and generosity. This is not given to you indefinitely. It is up to you to foster your boldness and greatness, and with every year I am learning how to grow up and out and love harder and deeper with less fear, less anger, and to always, always *be a sister*.

It's so important to show up for people
in need. To take someone in, to realize they
are struggling, and to inconvenience yourself
when you can save another person's day.
We all must remember that while we remain
the main character in our own story, sometimes
we are a supporting character in another's.

Baby on Board

I was twenty-six years old and on a plane ride home to New Jersey to visit my family for Christmas. I was sitting in first class, even though I was still waiting tables at this point in my life. Once I started flying first-class at the age of thirteen, there was no turning back. I didn't care how broke I was; I would always charge it and remind myself I'd be making more money once I became famous.

I sat down in my regular seat, 2C, and was followed moments later by a woman and her six-month-old baby. She put her baby down in the seat next to mine and then wrapped a seat belt around the child. The belt was quite baggy, considering plane seat belts are typically made for adults.

Once the baby was strapped in, the woman got up and sat in the seat in front of her own child.

"Um, excuse me?" I said, tapping her on the shoulder from my row behind her. "Would you like to switch seats so you can sit next to your baby?"

"No, thank you," she responded.

I was flummoxed. I looked at the baby. *Was this even allowed? Can a six-month-old sit alone on an airplane?*

I wasn't up to speed on the rules surrounding children flying, and

I was worried that if the mother was in front of the baby, then I would be left in charge, and wanted absolutely nothing to do with this whole situation.

When the flight attendant passed by, I nudged her and pointed at the baby. I could tell by the flight attendant's reaction that this was not common practice. She leaned down and whispered to me that she thought the baby's mother was having a bit of a hard time, and that maybe we should give her a minute.

I leaned forward again between the two seats and tapped the mother on the shoulder.

"Miss, don't you want to sit with your baby?" I asked her for a second time.

"Not right this minute."

"Okay, well, neither do I," I said, looking around for someone to help me out.

The flight attendant reappeared and informed the woman that babies that small weren't allowed to sit by themselves on airplanes, and while the seat next to me was empty, it wouldn't be possible for the baby to hang out by him- or herself. I couldn't tell what sex the baby was, because when I see babies, they all look fluid.

"I'm sorry, miss, but the baby needs to be in someone's lap for take-off," the flight attendant said.

When the woman got up to grab her baby in an angry haste, I saw tears running down her cheeks and smudging her mascara.

"I'll take it," I told the flight attendant, picking up the baby to put in my lap, realizing this woman was going through something, and did indeed need a minute. I thought of my mother and what she would have done in that situation. She would have gladly taken the baby and looked after it. The mother looked at me blankly and sat back down in her seat. She seemed almost in a trance. The baby was fine, a little too thin for my liking, because I was then and still am more attracted to meaty babies with lots of chunkiness and extra arm rolls. I peeked in its diaper and discovered the baby was a boy.

"Hello, little boy. Are you a little baby nugget?" I asked, nuzzling his neck. I rocked him back and forth and patted his back, and did all the other things I had seen mothers do. When the plane was finally in the air, I got up to give him back to his mother, only to discover that she was sound asleep.

I looked at the flight attendant, who asked me if I wanted her to wake the mother up. While that's exactly what I wanted, I thought it would be nicer to hold on to the baby until I couldn't handle it anymore. Here was an opportunity to give a stranger a hand, and even though I considered this a high-level inconvenience for me, it was the necessary gesture to help alleviate some stress for this woman, who was obviously going through something serious. I kept thinking of my own mother, and I did what I thought she would want me to do to help this woman.

I sat back down with my new baby and ordered a vodka soda. Then I ordered two more, and by the time we were descending into Newark, the baby was fast asleep in my arms, and I had a pretty solid buzz.

The woman in front of me woke up when we landed and she turned around to find her baby sleeping in my arms.

"Thank you."

"You're welcome."

Woman King

I f you are a woman between the ages of thirteen and forty-seven, and you sleep in the same bed as me, there is a 99 percent chance you will get your period the next morning.

My friend's thirteen-year-old daughter, Madeline, wanted to sleep in my bed with me.

"Only if you want to get your period," I told Madeline.

"I *do* want my period," she assured me. "All my friends have already gotten theirs."

The next morning, Maddy ran to the bathroom, and sure enough, she had become a woman.

"How do you do that?" Maddy's mom asked me.

"I'm not doing anything. I don't even have my period right now. It's just something that happens when young girls sleep in my bed. As unsettling as that sentence may sound."

My forty-five-year-old friend Ange hadn't gotten her period for a year, and when she shared a bed with me one night in Vegas, she screamed when she went to the bathroom.

"Fuck! What the fuck is this?"

"I told you not to sleep with me!" I yelled back.

"I thought this just happened when you slept with children who haven't gotten their periods!"

"Nope, it happens to all age groups," I told her.

I have given numerous young girls their periods; both of my sisters multiple times; and three women who had already entered menopause. Perhaps because I have chosen not to procreate, I have extra-powerful female hormones pumping through my veins, and with no release valve in the form of childbirth my fertility has no outlet.

My family and friends are aware of this phenomenon, and when discussing it, I've asked everyone to refer to me as the Woman King.

My brother Roy and I had to share a bed in Florida one Christmas. He offered to sleep on the floor. I told him I trusted him to not make a move on me, but he said he'd rather sleep on the floor than get his period.

Three years ago, my sister Simone told me she could start sleeping in bed with me again, because she had gotten an ablation, which is a procedure where they scorch your uterus to prevent any further bleeding. For 99 percent of women, this will prevent any additional bleeding, and the other 1 percent experience light spotting instead of a full period.

I had never heard of an ablation before, and immediately after Simone told me about this, I called my ob-gyn to schedule my own. The end of my period sounded dreamy.

My friend's daughter, whom we'll call Samantha, was fifteen and upset that she hadn't gotten her period. Her mother called me and asked if I could come to Florida to pay a visit and give her daughter her first period. I try to avoid Florida at all costs, plus I was no longer menstruating, so I wasn't sure that I could trigger it in others. I told my friend that I had gotten an ablation and didn't know if I still had the power.

"The irony," she said. "Here we are trying to get rid of our periods, and now I have a daughter dying to start hers. It's getting pretty desperate around here. We'll come to you."

My friend and her daughter flew to St. Louis to see one of my stand-up shows, and after my show we went back to the hotel room. I felt slightly cringey patting my bed and telling Samantha to hop in.

"Is there anything special I need to do?" she asked, looking up at me like a deer in the headlights. I felt like Bill Cosby.

"No, honey. I don't want you to get your hopes up, because I don't even know if I have the power anymore. Just hold my hand when we go to sleep. That's all we can do."

Guess who woke up with their period?

Not me.

Katelyn

once had an intervention with a woman I barely knew. She had been to my house only a few times, but in every instance she had been on drugs, alcohol, and who knows what else. I am very open to all of these behaviors as long as that person isn't a drain or a mess or someone who ends up passing out on my bathroom floor.

This woman was all three of those things, and when I asked her close circle of friends what the game plan for her intervention was, they looked at each other and then explained to me how difficult it was to hang out with her and that it might just be easier moving forward to not include her. That seemed like the saddest, least effective nonsolution to a problem that was only going to get worse, so I picked up the phone and called her myself.

She came over to my house that afternoon. When she arrived, I made her a cocktail, sat her down on the balcony of my bedroom, and gave it to her straight.

I told her about her behavior that I had witnessed, and I said that because of this she was driving the people who loved her away. I also suggested that maybe she was capable of toning it down rather than getting sober, as I have certainly had times in my own life when I had taken things too far, and I had to recalibrate.

"Listen," I said to her. "I like to drink and party, too. But if your behavior while doing those things is more consistently bad than good, something has to give. You're going to lose your friends and possibly your family. I know you may be hurt and embarrassed by this, but as a woman it is my duty to be honest with you. I don't want to see any of these things happen to you, and as someone who is not in your inner circle, I really have no agenda here. My only agenda is sisterhood."

She seemed shocked and slightly mortified and apologized for her behavior. I also told her that it wasn't necessary to apologize to me, that I would always remain her friend, but if I were in her shoes, I'd want someone to be honest with me and tell me the truth.

This acquaintance ended up going to rehab a couple of years later when her real circle of friends finally came together to show up for her and do a proper intervention.

I got an email from her while she was away in that program thanking me for my honesty and telling me she hadn't been in a place to hear it at the time, but that it had planted the seed for her to come to understand that there would eventually have to be an end to her drinking.

When she got home from that rehab program, we went for a walk and she told me that everyone in rehab was asked to share the story of the first person who told them they had a problem. When it was her turn, she announced to the group that Chelsea Handler was the person who first told her she had a drinking problem; she said she had never made that many people laugh before.

After her group leader caught her breath from the idea of me telling someone they had a drug and alcohol problem, she said to the group, "If Chelsea Handler says you have a problem, you probably better listen."

My friend has been sober for three years now, and she is happier and healthier than ever.

Sisterhood.

Road Trip

After my dog Bert passed away, I was one dog down and had Bernice all to myself. My relationship with Bernice had always been strained. Due to his voluptuous body type, Bert had always been the apple of my eye. Like many dogs who lose a sibling, Bernice pepped up big-time once Bert was out of the picture. She, like many females, had been marginalized by her brother and my affection for him. She spent her life having zero to little interest in any leftover affection I might be offering her, and then add my being on tour, she saw me on average three days every two weeks. Neglect.

The rest of the time she spent living with my housekeeper, Mabel, and having a love affair with Mabel's fourteen-year-old son, Fernando. While I was on tour, Mabel would send me licentious pictures of Bernice under the covers in Fernando's bed, or Bernice sitting in Fernando's lap at a basketball game. I suspected these photos were staged because Bernice would never sit in my lap or get under the covers in my bed, and add to that, Mabel loves to make me jealous. I had always presumed that Bert and Bernice hailed from Mexico, because they seemed to understand Spanish better than English, but who knew what kind of Scooby snacks Mabel was bribing them with when they were in her care. It was my job as a parent to break this cycle.

I had time off coming up and I wanted to use it to show up for Bernice, to work on our Spanish together, and to be a real mother. I wanted her under *my* covers and sitting in *my* lap. I was headed to Whistler for my winter ski break and I thought it would be the perfect time for a road trip with Bernice. She was getting old and I thought this might be my last winter with her, so I wanted to make sure she felt loved and protected by me as she transitioned out of this world into Bert's afterlife arms.

The reaction that my friends, family, and staff had to the idea of me driving from Los Angeles to Whistler was embarrassing. Everyone I told was shocked.

"You're going to drive all the way to Canada? Alone? That's not a good idea, Chelsea," my girlfriend told me.

"Why? I know how to drive, and I'm quite looking forward to it. Three days alone with Bernice. Not talking to anyone. That sounds heavenly."

"I can't wait to see what kind of trouble you get into all by yourself. I wonder how far you'll make it before you order a plane," my cousin Molly told me.

The man who takes my dogs for a walk every morning is named Felix. He takes care of all the outdoor stuff at my house along with my cars and any electronic stuff inside my house, which is an everlasting problem for me. Sonos specifically is a nemesis of mine, and along with half the population I fantasize about suing them one day. Felix sat with me in the Ford SUV that we rented for my trip and he slowly explained to me how to sync my phone to the airplay. He also informed me that when the gas gauge gets below one-half of a tank, it is time to get gas. In my defense, I do drive an electric car, but the idea that they believe I am so remedial that I'm not aware of when to get gas is preposterous.

Ange called me from Whistler when she heard I was driving and said, "Buddy, I don't think this is a good idea. Why don't I meet you in Portland?" My sister had messaged her that I was driving alone and was concerned. It was absolutely ludicrous. There are things I can't do, like cook, or sew, or browse websites, but I've been driving since I was twelve.

As usual, everyone's concern only motivated me more, and I knew that the three days would allow me some one-on-one time with Bernice so she could forget Mabel, Fernando, Felix, and all the other Mexican people in her life she preferred over me. It would also give my face time to heal before I crossed the border into Canada.

In celebration of having one month off until I had to work again, I had elected for another CO_2 laser facial treatment, which meant that I could not be seen in daylight. Not because I'm famous, but because I looked battered. I had my wide-brimmed Bruce Springsteen trucker hat on as well as sunglasses, so it was hard to make out what exactly was going on with my face, but underneath the getup it was peeling, bruised, and swollen. If I was outside L.A. and saw a woman driving around with a face like that, I would call the police.

Bernice and I drove from L.A. to Bend, Oregon, and visited a friend of mine there. She had invited us to stay at her house, but I wasn't going to expose her four children to my third-degree burns, so I opted for a hotel. Somehow in the day it took me to get to Oregon, my cheeks had ballooned to twice their normal size, and now I looked like Rocky Dennis in the movie *Mask*. When I texted a picture to my aesthetician who performed the treatment, she told me to pick up some vinegar rinses from a Rite Aid or CVS.

I texted her back, "I'm not about to go into a store looking like this. A gas station, maybe, but nothing more sophisticated than that."

I was checking into hotels at night, so that was less of an issue with my baseball hat and sunglasses on. This was by far the most ravaged I had ever looked after a laser. I had done a CO_2 on my eyes before, but this time I did my entire face, and I looked positively unstable. Bernice, on the other hand, had never looked more adorable. I had her hair shorn before we left for Whistler, so she looked like a combination of a little sheep and a baby bear, with the sweetest little innocent-looking teddy bear eyes. When people see her, they always think she's a puppy.

The problem with Bernice is that she attracts a lot of attention, which can be annoying when a dog walks less than one mile per hour, because that's a lot of people you have to interact with. So, when anyone asked if they could pet her, I pretended I only spoke Spanish and that she did, too. We spent our days driving and then pulling off into rest areas, where she could stroll and eat. Since Bernice's snail-like pace prevents any sudden movement, I'd sit and watch her sniff her way around, look back to make sure I was there—which gave me immense pride—and sniff around some more. When people or other dogs would approach her, she would pivot and walk in the opposite direction. Bernice is a bitch. She doesn't take any crap from anyone, and she will never be polite to make anyone feel better. She is her own woman, and this, too, fills me with a great deal of maternal pride.

I tried to listen to a mindless murder mystery audiobook, but I'm not very good at listening to books, because my mind wanders. I need a book in my hand to read and absorb. Bernice also had little interest in the audiobook, probably because she speaks Spanish, plus, the scenery was so beautiful. We both spent a lot of time focusing on that. I had missed so much nature growing up. I spent my youth being outside, but never appreciating it. Never stopping to soak in the beauty of the trees, the lush greenery, and all the little societies that live within our forests. Meditation taught me a lot about appreciating the natural beauty that is almost everywhere you look, and when walking any dog, to notice what they are taking in, being patient, and letting them wander and explore. This was another opportunity for me to change my behavior and walk Bernice every few hours and feed her, which are two things I can't say I do very often.

My life in L.A. is like having four personal nannies who are there when I wake up and are shepherding me throughout the day. I rarely do anything for myself when I'm in L.A., and that's the way I like it. Going to Whistler is different. That's one of the reasons I love it so much. I like being in charge of groceries, dog walking, laundry, errands, and being a normal person.

When the pouring rain turned into pelting rain, I decided a break for some gas would be a good idea. I stopped, got out of the car, put my credit card in the machine, and clicked down on the pump, then took Bernice for a little walk. She absolutely loves the rain because she is her mother's daughter, and I could sit and watch the rain for hours. She will sit in the rain or the snow and just chill—like a little bear. No one in Los Angeles seems to appreciate the break in the weather, and when people talk about the high rate of suicides in Oregon and Seattle due to the unrelenting rain, I always think about how many books I could write if I lived somewhere where it rained for months at a time.

I got back in the car and was driving for another twenty minutes before my gas light went on telling me I was low on gas. *Huh?* I had just filled up my tank, or did I? *Jesus. Fuck me.* I didn't even check to see if the tank had filled up; it was clear that I was out of practice at pumping gas. I wasn't about to turn back and drive another twenty minutes to the gas station that I couldn't remember, so I looked for the next one, and when I got there, I couldn't find the credit card I'd used at the last place. Then I did the same exact thing at this gas station: I put my credit card in, clicked on the pump, and as I was driving away, I realized I still had no gas, and once again I had left another credit card there. So, not only did I pay for two empty tanks of gas, I left two different credit cards at two different gas stations. Maybe Felix hadn't been that far off with my remedial directions regarding gas, after all. Many people would have gone back for their credit cards, but that is not my style.

Driving through the pouring rain, through the lush forests that line Oregon, about to run out of gas, I felt my soul filling up with sunshine. The overwhelming feeling of freedom in driving up to Canada with my dog, knowing I was headed to the place that fills me up with so much. Real gratitude for getting my life together and understanding that all this happiness and gratitude is my reward for taking the time to get to know myself. Grateful for all the decisions that led me to this point. Grateful I took the time to find out that skiing makes me so happy. Grateful that I went after my happiness like my life depended on it, because it did. The time spent in therapy, the time after therapy, and the calm and patience I have gained through growth and learning more and doing better. No one is unrecoverable. You can change your life anytime you want.

Anytime anyone called or texted me to check in, I would respond by letting them know I was camping and would be in and out of cell service.

By the time we checked into the Four Seasons in Seattle, Bernice and I were attached, except for the fact that I kept calling her Denise. I'm not sure why that was happening, because I don't even have a Denise in my life. But Bernice is also deaf, so I'm not sure she even gives a shit.

The valet at the Four Seasons gave me a map of different dog parks in the area, but I feel the same way about dog parks as I feel about men with long fingernails: no thank you. I've had some of my worst interactions with human beings at dog parks.

Instead, I had secured a BabyBjörn and strapped Bernice onto the front of my chest anytime we needed to go for a long walk to find some grass, because downtown Seattle has no grassy areas anywhere. This, too, became an issue because everyone and their mother wanted to stop and say hello to Bernice, but it was dark out, so I kept my face low and hidden under my hat. Bernice can take up to one hour to walk fifteen feet, and while that can be laborious, the flip side is that, just like her mother, she hates water, so she pees only twice a day.

After our walk that night, I decided to hit the gym at the Four Seasons and walked in with Bernice in her BabyBjörn. The extra thirty-four pounds was a great added weight for my squats and walking lunges. I could see by the head jerk of the only other woman working out that she recognized me and that it wouldn't be possible to avoid an interaction.

"Chelsea Handler!" she said. "I'm from New Jersey, too!"

"Oh, really?" I asked. "What are you doing in Seattle?"

"My son just had bottom surgery!" she exclaimed, proudly.

"Oh, wow," I said, smiling. "I just had a CO_2 laser on my face." Sometimes, things fly out of my mouth that are so stupid there is almost no point in addressing them. I just try to move the conversation on as quickly as possible in an effort to make up for it in the next part of our exchange. Make a new impression to replace the last one is how I like to think of it. The woman told me her son was a big fan and that he listened to my podcast, *Dear Chelsea,* every week.

"Where is he?" I asked her, implying I'd like to meet him, my attempt at covering up my earlier idiotic comment.

"He's still in the hospital. He'll be there for a few more days."

"Well, let's get a picture together for him," I told her.

"Really?" she asked, looking at my face, which was now shedding skin, revealing bright red patches underneath. So, now there is a photo out there somewhere with this boy's mother and me looking like I just escaped a fire.

That night in Seattle, Bernice came up to the side of my bed and placed her little paws right on the edge until I picked her up and put her into bed with me. This is what I had been dreaming about. I have spent her entire life trapping her in my bed, only for her to play dead and go to her safe place until the assault is over and then scramble away the minute she thinks I'm done. Her putting her paws up on the bed frame was just about the cutest thing I had ever seen. She was finally returning my affection and I didn't care that it was because I was the only one there. Spending those three days in the car with her was all she needed to know that I was there for her; I was present and going to take care of her. My parenting comes in bursts, and with any consistency its rewards are bountiful. My efforts had paid off, and she knew I was her mama.

The next morning, we got up bright and early and hit the Canadian border. I saw a female agent in one of the lanes and tried to squeeze in there, because she would more easily understand what I had done to my face, and it wasn't something that could be overlooked. Unfortunately, I got stuck in a lane where there were two males working the booth.

"Hello," I said to the two male officers. "I had my skin lasered off, so that's what's happening here." I gestured to my face. They both looked at me and then at each other and had zero reaction to the crust that had formed all over my face. "What are you doing in Canada?" the guy standing in the window asked me, ignoring my earlier statement.

"Skiing. I have a house in Whistler."

"Are you bringing anything into the country, like alcohol, cannabis, or firearms?"

"I do not have any guns," I told them, focusing on the one thing they mentioned that I wasn't in possession of.

I have a good relationship with the Canadian border. I keep the most crucial information to myself, and they seem perfectly fine being lied to.

By the time we arrived at my place in Whistler, Bernice was lying with her head in my lap. Her being away from all her helpers in L.A. made her realize I was the only option left, and she leaned in and accepted that everyone else she had grown to trust was a distant memory.

Where she had once rebuffed my advances to pick her up, or would walk away when I tried to pet her, she would now walk over to me and park herself next to me, press in on my hand when I petted her, and nuzzle in my armpit when I carried her. Before, I would accost her, lift her up into my arms, and make her sit on my lap for as long as she would have it. First, she would submit, play dead, but when things calmed down, she'd open her eyes to see if the assault was still happening, and when she realized it was, she'd close them tight to avoid making eye contact. Now she was leaning into me, nuzzling my face to kiss her—acting like a very affectionate cat.

We were finally vibing, and I had so much love to shower her with.

After I had provided her with consistency and security, she was able to soften into me, knowing I was sticking around—that this wasn't a month of touring where I would be bopping in and out of her life.

When I walked into my Whistler house, I found my kitchen counter covered with every sort of edible and chocolate mushroom you could dream up. Chocolate with MDMA, mushroom chocolate, chocolate with LSD, every imaginable combination of chocolate with pretty much anything you can do with chocolate. After all my time here, I have made a great group of friends who had all dropped off food, drugs, and soup at my house for my arrival. There was even a stack of fresh books my friend had collected for me. I had made myself a little slice of heaven. A place I go to be me. To get away from the noise of my real life. The warmth of my little village life in Whistler. My favorite place to be. At home in my village, where I'm a villager. It's my happiest place on earth, my Disneyland.

After five full days of round-the-clock parenting, I was exhausted. The great thing about my neighborhood in Whistler is that it's private and small, so with Bernice's new Apple AirTag, I just started letting her out the front door on her own. When Bernice wanted to go outside, I would open my front door, let her out, and then track her on my phone about fifteen minutes later. She was never more than twenty feet from the house. I thought this was a very reasonable solution to me walking outside and standing next to her while she sniffed other dogs' urine for twenty minutes.

On day three of this routine, I must have lost track of time, because when I tracked her on Find My Friends, she was across the street in a completely different development, which meant she had crossed traffic. *Oh my God.* I hauled ass out my door and ran up the hill and across the street. I'd had a knee scope two months earlier, so my running was not anything that I would take pleasure in having other people see. Once across the street, I gimped over to where my phone said Bernice would be. That's when I heard a little boy on his balcony, yelling to his father.

"Daddy, come outside. There's a baby bear walking around looking for his mama."

"I'm right here! I'm her mama!" I screamed, breathlessly limping around the corner. Bernice didn't have her handkerchief on this time, so I forgave the confusion. Also, the mistake was coming from a little boy, and we all know how children tug at my heart.

I had no idea Bernice had it in her to cross the street on her own. Who knew how many other skills she had I didn't know about? Could she also type?

"What a mysterious little bear you are," I told her, as I threw her over my shoulder. "Mommy is so sorry for being so bad at being a mommy. The good news is, I have so much room for improvement!"

The minute I loosened my reins on her parenting, Bernice made it clear she wasn't going to tolerate that behavior from her mother.

It was the same thing I had learned with Poopsie, Whoopsie, and Oopsie. They want to be parented. They desire structure and routine and consistency in order to feel safe and secure, and when the parent gets lazy, the child becomes obstinate and then acts out for your attention. I needed to apply all my parenting knowledge to my own dog, and she was telling me that she wanted me by her side. She wanted to be looked after, and I needed to meet the moment and level up.

Two steps forward, one step back.

Learning the art of making an argument without yelling or screaming is something to behold. I've always dreamed of becoming the kind of person who can do that. Nothing feels like winning more than not losing your temper.

Boundaries

I had a friend tell me that while my generosity was greatly appreciated, it shouldn't be given with the expectation that it be returned. This was coming from someone who claimed their bandwidth didn't allow them to give of their time and energy in a way that matched what I was giving of mine. This friend believed that everyone should be accepted where they are and that not everyone is capable of the same giving.

"*Giving*," he said, "is really only *giving* when you don't feel like doing it." It dawned on me in that moment that he believed *giving* came more easily to me. While this may be partially true, I'm not always in the mood to jump up and help people or lend a hand, but the more I've practiced it, the more of an instinct it has become. And, now I was learning, the easier it will seem to others.

One day, this same friend, whom we'll call Dean, told me that one of our mutual friends—let's call her Rachel—a person he had been friends with for twenty years and someone I had known very casually for five, was going through a difficult divorce and needed help.

"I told her to call you, Chels. You're better in a crisis than I am. I hope that's okay."

"Okay," I said. "But, I don't know Rachel that well. I don't know that she's going to feel comfortable with my help in this."

"I just can't deal with it. I have too much going on," Dean said.

I, too, had a lot going on during this time, but I sensed that Dean was having personal issues of his own, which prevented him from being available to Rachel. He had been unavailable to me for months. Each time I had tried to broach the topic with him, it was clear he was not interested in acknowledging that anything was wrong. In fact, it seemed he didn't believe there was any problem at all.

"Sure," I told Dean. "If Rachel reaches out, I'll be there. Of course."

She did reach out, and I made it my business to help her through an extremely difficult and traumatizing divorce. Through this period, Dean checked in with her only occasionally; he seemed more preoccupied with some new friends he had made.

This became visible to Rachel, but I falsely assured her that Dean would show up when it was time for him to—even though I had a feeling in my gut that he wouldn't. My relationship with Dean had been strained for some time, and now I was seeing him treat another old friend the same way he had been treating me. I don't normally put up with this kind of behavior from friends, but my relationship with Dean had been long and complex. He had gone through a pretty dreadful breakup years earlier and had leaned on me, heavily. I made it my personal mission to get him up off the floor and back on his feet, to help him financially, professionally, emotionally, to do whatever it took to get his confidence and well-being back on track. For many years after that, I felt personally responsible for his happiness, and our relationship turned into a pretty codependent one. If there was any issue at all, he'd come to me, and I'd drop everything to help fix it. Then, when it was time for him to be happy for my growth and learning after therapy, he didn't show up.

Dean didn't believe in many of the things I had started taking more seriously—like meditation, energy, or that there was a universal intelligence. His stance was that anyone who believed in God was an idiot, that nothing happens for a reason, and that we are all a bunch of ants marching along. He also had a hard time being happy for anyone else's achievements, including mine. He could be negative and unkind; I hated to admit this, but throughout our friendship I had allowed many of his thoughts to influence my own.

It felt like Dean didn't appreciate that I didn't want to sit around and gossip all day long anymore, or that I was calmer, quieter, and more circumspect about almost everything. He looked away when I had good news to share or turned away when I asked him to talk about what was going on. I booked an appointment with my therapist Dan to discuss how to handle it, and to see if there was any hope at all for a recovery; maybe this was just a rough patch in a very long friendship.

I wanted to be careful around this issue. Before therapy, I had a long history of leaving friendships in the dust, along with a field of debris when the relationship ended. At times, I have gone through friends, lovers, and colleagues like a hurricane, with little sentimentality when the relationships ended. I didn't want to do that anymore.

This friendship was different. Dean and I had been through so much together; we'd weathered so many tough times, done so much hand-holding, shared so much laughter and so many memories.

Now it felt like the contour of our friendship had changed, and what once was, was no longer. It no longer felt comforting or fun to spend time together. It felt forced, obligatory, unsafe. He had in fact been a good friend on many occasions, but there seemed to be a very evident lopsidedness to our friendship in its current form. I had started to see behavior from him that didn't add up to the person I thought he was. It took a long time for me to admit—we had lost our chemistry.

"Play better chess" was a favorite line of his whenever I ended a friendship or work relationship or shut the door on someone I'd fallen out with.

"I'm not playing chess," I would tell him, over and over again. He would respond by telling me that I needed to be more strategic.

I didn't understand the strategy with which he looked at everything. I didn't want to be "strategic" in my friendships, and I didn't want to "work it" with someone I didn't like or want to spend time with just because they were "powerful" or could help my career. I couldn't be that kind of person if I tried. I don't kiss ass, and I don't angle to befriend people because they might be "valuable" down the road. I started seeing Dean operate in a way that made me question almost everything I had thought to be true about him, and it felt very much at times like he was climbing over my back to get to better people, and that I had in fact lost my value.

My therapist Dan suggested that I bring Dean into therapy to discuss the changes in our friendship. I didn't think that would be a fruitful experience, but he did guide me in having an evenhanded private conversation with Dean about the actions of his that had so hurt me. Dan told me to come from a place of love, to make it a conversation, not an argument. To be still and calm, and put all my new learnings from therapy to use in having a constructive conversation with a loved one that didn't lead to an argument.

So, that's what I did. One afternoon, I invited Dean over to my house and we sat on my deck and I told him that I had felt hurt over some of the interactions that had transpired between us. This conversation happened not long after Dean had flown to Whistler to celebrate my birthday. He behaved terribly the entire trip, complaining about everyone from the driver to our ski guides; almost everything was met with his contempt. It was obvious from his behavior that he didn't want to be there and that he resented the fact that he felt obligated to come.

In our conversation, I shared other, smaller examples of stuff that felt very icky, and I asked if he understood how this kind of behavior was affecting me. We sat on my deck and he seemed genuinely sorry for having upset me, taking responsibility and apologizing for all of it. He assured me it was never his intent to hurt me. When he left my house that day, I didn't know where our relationship was headed. The apology could have been sincere, or pat. I didn't know, but I wanted to act with integrity, and for me having integrity means being up-front.

I returned to Whistler for a few weeks of skiing, and a couple of days later, while I was skiing down my favorite run, I got a call from Rachel, who by this point had become a close friend of mine. Rachel was in tears because Dean and I had both agreed to write letters of support in her divorce case. Rachel said that Dean had pulled his original letter and reworked it after finding out that her ex would be made aware of the letter. Dean's new husband had worked professionally with Rachel's ex on a few projects, and it was evident from Dean's reworked letter that he did not want to jeopardize that relationship. It was also obvious that the letter had been rewritten by Dean's new husband.

I had my own issues with Dean, but watching how this affected Rachel made me sick to my stomach. Dean had been through a similarly unpleasant divorce just a couple years earlier, and he had needed similar letters of support from his closest friends and family. He had walked in Rachel's shoes; he had experienced firsthand the ugliness of a bad breakup, and I had been there for him every step of the way. And now, when an opportunity arose for him to return that love and support to someone in need, he bailed. He and his partner were so obviously acting in their own best interest while our friend was scared and unsure about her future.

I sat in the middle of the ski run and texted Dean and his new husband and let them know this new letter wasn't going to fly. I said that we needed to have a conversation on Zoom with Rachel. I wanted them to see Rachel face-to-face, and she asked me to be there to support her and help guide the conversation. I didn't appreciate that my friendship with Rachel had been a result of Dean's lack of interest or availability, and I was infuriated that I now had to be the one to knock some sense into him on behalf of the friend he had assigned to me.

The Zoom resulted in Rachel explaining to both of them how shocking their revision of their letter of support had been, to which they appropriately apologized, but also played dumb. When we were ending the conversation, I relayed to both Dean and his partner that it seemed their self-interest had become a pattern of behavior, as I had just spoken to Dean about this very topic weeks prior. They didn't like that.

Ten minutes after I got off the Zoom, I received an email from Dean telling me that he and I needed to take a break from our relationship. He said that I seemed constantly disappointed in him, and that everything he had apologized for at my house in L.A. had actually never happened—that I had imagined most of what we discussed, denying my entire experience in our friendship.

"Save your honesty for us," Dean had told me ad infinitum over the years, referring to him and his new husband, reminding me that most people preferred not to be confronted, or to be told the truth, or any of the other behaviors I was well known for doling out. But after reading Dean's email, I realized that the very people for whom I was supposed to save the truth were not actually interested at all in hearing it. I knew that getting on that Zoom and standing up for my friend would end our relationship. I also knew that it would result in Rachel getting the original letter that Dean had written on her behalf. And I was right on both counts: Rachel got her letter, and Dean's and my friendship came to its natural end.

There will be many surprises in how people react to your own personal transformation and betterment. These are not obstacles, and you do not have to react to these instances with resistance. You have a choice to take everything in grace. Accept, accept, accept. When people tell you they need space, give it to them. When people tell you they are not happy for you or that they're not on your side, be grateful to have that knowledge.

I lost a close friend that day. I also gained Rachel, who is kind, gracious, caring, and always present, and who has had a complete transformation since her divorce. She is strong, grounded, and clear about who she is and what she's looking for. She has shown up for me in endless ways since that day. From this new friendship, I have been given everything I was missing in my relationship with Dean.

Not everyone is meant to be in your life forever. Some people are only here to get you from one chapter to the next, and sometimes you are the person helping someone get from one chapter to the next. Be grateful for the experience and be graceful when it's over.

Telling people the truth can be an unpopular thing to do, and while I have lost friendships because of it, it won't ever stop me from giving people my honest opinion. Telling the truth to the people you love, especially when it's inconvenient, is honorable. There should be more honesty in this world, not less. If someone is flailing, floundering, or not seeing something clearly, it is important for them to hear the truth. There have been so many instances in my life where no one told me that I was dating an asshole, or that I was being unreasonable, or that I had behaved badly. The times when someone did, I have relished. I have listened, adjusted my behavior accordingly, and made improvements. These people who have told me the truth will be in my life for as long as they want. I am grateful for the truth, as hard as it may be to bear—it is a gift.

These are the moments when life begins again. It's another launch, a fresh lens into a reality you weren't expecting. The loss of one thing means gaining another. Accept the truth, the change that comes with the truth, and the warmth of knowing that you showed up for someone when they needed you the most. You didn't turn away.

Be honest about who you are, and let people decide if they like you. And be less selfish. Selfishness never led to a good ending. It's the worst part of every story. It's so much cooler to be generous, even when you feel like you don't have much to share.

Showing Up

To know when someone is at their worst, and to lean in.

To see them at their most terrible, and to stick.

To call them out, to be unafraid.

To know the truth is what you said.

To say *hello.*

To say *I know.*

To let you go.

I will always think of you with a dimple on your cheek. And I will always think of us like a beautiful winning streak.

You gave me good, I gave you better, you took it back, you made me never . . . want to give up on telling the truth.

Woody Allen

Years ago, I accidentally ended up at a dinner party in New York City sitting across from Woody Allen and Soon-Yi Previn. I started clicking my knees together, flabbergasted that I was seated directly across from a man and his daughter/bride. On the one hand, I didn't want to make a scene, because there were eight other people at this dinner party; on the other hand, there was no way as a woman that I was not going to say something. So, I waited.

I remained perfectly pleasant throughout the several courses of dinner and made sure I spoke to everyone evenly and I bided my time. I even asked Woody Allen and Soon-Yi several questions about themselves that were unrelated to them being married. I asked him about directing the movie *Annie*, which I had confused with *Annie Hall*, the movie he did actually direct. I get away with a lot of missteps like this because people think I'm joking, but in many instances I generally have no idea what I'm talking about.

Just wait, I kept telling myself. *Patience truly is a virtue.* I was exercising that virtue consciously and with a purpose. And that's what I did. I waited a full two hours until the dessert was served, and as Woody Allen was taking his first bite out of his blackberry cobbler, I leaned into the two of them and asked, "So, how did *you two* meet?"

I slept like a baby that night.

When you see something, you *must* say something. You must. That is what sisterhood is. Never looking away, never apologizing to or accommodating men who are powerful, and making sure every time you leave a room, everyone knows you were there and what it is you stand for.

The Trouble
with Men

O ne sunny California weekday, I pulled up to the nail salon
I like to go to on Montana Avenue in Santa Monica.

This is a street with parking meters, so I parallel
parked my car next to a parking meter—which I chose to ignore.

When I got out of my car and headed toward the nail salon, a guy
on the sidewalk yelled out to me, "Hey, you didn't feed the meter!"

I've had trouble with men my whole life. Either they want to control me, or they are repelled by my unwillingness to be controlled.
Regardless, they have been a problem for me for quite some time.
While I remain sexually attracted to the male species, I do believe
they are becoming harder and harder to have sex with.

"I'm sorry?" I asked, in order to confirm that this man was indeed
talking to me.

"I was just telling you that you didn't feed the meter." He wasn't
unpleasant; he actually seemed nice. So, I matched his tone and even
took it to the next level. I became upbeat.

"Yeah, I know. I'm the one who just did it," I said with a big friendly
smile, as I stood across from him trying to grasp how someone could

be so invested in controlling a situation he had nothing to do with. I was genuinely curious, and made sure I remained overly friendly.

"You're gonna get a ticket," he informed me.

"Maybe," I said, shrugging. "But, I think you're confusing me with someone who gives a shit," I said, smiling with big eyes.

"Oh, you don't *care* if you get a ticket?" He said this with the first hint of mockery in his voice as if he didn't believe I didn't care. As if someone would *pretend* that they didn't care about putting money in a parking meter. For what purpose? To show off?

"But, I don't *care* if I get a ticket," I assured him, cheerfully, to let him know I wasn't being cantankerous. I felt slightly crazy the way I had to contort my face by overly emoting positive vibes in the hopes that this man wouldn't feel attacked. I could see the kindness in his eyes; I believed this man had potential. I felt like a conversation with me would be a worthwhile exchange and that maybe I could help him grasp how unnecessary men's behavior can feel toward women. After all, if I hadn't believed in his potential, I wouldn't have wasted my time.

I like to serve it up to people, but I don't get off on it. Just like I didn't set out to embarrass Piers Morgan when I was on his CNN show many years ago by telling him he was a terrible interviewer. He embarrassed himself by not paying attention to the person he was interviewing. Had he done his homework, he would have known I wasn't going to put up with a man looking at his phone while interviewing me. Piers Morgan has proven himself to be an absolute upside-down moron, but I could tell that this man wasn't.

I feel most times when I take the time to actually chat with an interloper like this, I am providing a service to the stupid and ignorant. With their newfound knowledge, there's a chance that their behavior can improve.

"Sir, I think you and I should have a talk."

He stared at me for a minute, trying to figure out how he knew me.

"I'm Chelsea," I said, putting out my hand. "What's your name?"

"I'm Lou," he said, putting out his. "Are you the comedian?"

"Yes, that's the one. I'd like to talk to you about what you just did. I'd like to help you."

"Oh, you're the one who hates children and hates men," he said to me.

My experience with children is twofold: I absolutely love kids who are polite and engaging and have manners. I do not appreciate the other kind. I do not blame any child for their behavior; I blame their parents. I blame men for men.

"Well, I don't hate children, and I don't hate men. I just think both can be very exhausting."

"Well, that's pretty sexist," he told me. This made me smile.

The person who has never experienced sexism in their life cannot start complaining about it as soon as they hear of the concept. You don't get to tell the gender that has been discriminated against since the beginning of time that they're being sexist.

"I want you to think about what you just said, and then think if you are being reasonable right now," I said, smiling. My composure in this situation was new and I was digging it. Years before, I would have gone off on this guy, but keeping a measured and agreeable tone is a big help in making a point.

"I was just trying to help you out, and now you're attacking me," Lou said.

"How so, Lou? I'm standing across from you engaged in a conversation with you about *me* being sexist because you needed to alert me that I hadn't fed the meter. Who is being sexist?"

He stared at me. I waited for something to click in him because he seemed young enough that with the right direction his behavior and attitude could improve. After all, when someone explains something to me that I don't know, I appreciate the time they took with me—but I'm also a woman.

"Lou, as helpful as you think you're being, I am not your responsibility. My car is not your responsibility. I don't even know you. I'm curious. Do you think I don't know about parking meters? Do you think this is my very first parking experience? And furthermore, why are my actions of any concern to you? Why are you calling me sexist?"

He stared at me some more and seemed bemused. I held on to my very calm tone while also challenging him, and this confused him.

"I'm very curious to know what you think about what I'm saying to you right now."

He stared at me some more. I put my hand on his upper arm to let him know I wasn't arguing. I wanted to connect.

"I don't know," he said. "I was just trying to help you."

"Were you, though? Would you have said that to a man?"

"Of course."

"And how do you think a grown man would have reacted to you telling him he hadn't fed his parking meter when it was standing there in plain sight?"

Silence, searching, and then, "Ah . . ."

I smiled at him. I thought about kissing him on the cheek, but didn't want to throw him off-balance.

"You're a good man to realize that *we, women,* are just so tired of being told what to do. You have to appreciate how annoying it is for us. I didn't feed the meter, because I forgot something upstairs in the nail salon and I'll be back in two minutes, and I don't need to be told by a strange man who is not a meter maid to follow the rules. It's not the biggest deal in the world, but it's a micro-annoyance, and if you have a few of those a day, it becomes a macro-annoyance and then it becomes chronic, and we just don't want to have to keep explaining ourselves. Do you understand where I'm coming from, Lou?"

"Yeah," he said. "I guess I do."

People always tell me I am wasting my time with conversations like this and sometimes I am. But not this time. My instincts were right. This man was worth the time. Even though telling someone to feed their meter is a minor infraction—and some would even say he was being thoughtful—I chose to look at it as a teaching moment. It's not men's fault that they are constantly instructing us. That's what they've been taught, and what we've allowed because none of us knew better. Now we do. So, having that kind of thoughtful exchange without yelling or losing your shit can be impactful. If the men who have potential aren't alerted to their pathological behavior, there is a danger they will become extinct.

It's already happening with animals. It's a phenomenon called parthenogenesis, where female animals procreate without help or semen from male animals. It happened to an anaconda in a zoo, a falcon, a shark, and a crocodile. We are typically one thousand years behind animals. So, if men aren't careful, the one thing we need from them in order to make the world go round might not be necessary anymore. If that happens, what would be the point of straight men? I would hate for men to become extinct, and that's why I'm only trying to help.

Exes and My Big Mouth

One early summer afternoon, I was walking downtown in New York City to meet some friends for lunch. I had a new Apple Watch on my wrist that wouldn't stop buzzing. Along with all other technology, I didn't yet know how to work my Apple Watch, and from what I could tell, it was set to supply me only with the information I am the least interested in knowing about. Every time I tried to turn on music or check my texts or emails, I was alerted in neon bold type about which direction I was headed in, north, northwest, south, southwest. If I wanted a compass, I would have bought one at a jewelry store like a normal person. When the buzzing alert for emails started overriding my compass setting, I grabbed my phone out of my pocket to get a better look at my emails. My ex Ted Harbert—a man I had dated when I was in my early thirties—had sent an email that read, "Some things are better left private. Please don't do that again."

That was a pretty brusque email to get from him. I had no idea what he was talking about, so I stopped mid-stride and tried to figure out what he could be referring to. Had I done something new or said something publicly? When nothing came to mind, I googled myself. That's when I got my first fifty clues. There were dozens of news hits, starting with Page Six from the *New York Post,* with the headline CHELSEA HANDLER RECALLS THREESOME WITH MASSEUSE THAT LED TO BREAKUP WITH EX.

Shitskydoodle.

My memory had been jogged. I had been on Andy Cohen's radio show the previous morning and, by the time I met a friend for breakfast afterward, had completely forgotten I had even been on a radio show. When Andy Cohen asked me if I had ever had a threesome, I told him that I had indeed had several with a masseuse and my exboyfriend Ted Harbert. I also added that I knew the relationship was over because I started calling the masseuse when Ted was out of town.

Double shitskydoodle.

Ted was living in Ecuador with his new wife, so it never occurred to me that he would even hear about my interview on Andy Cohen— or that I was even telling another person's story . . . again. This was becoming a hard habit to break.

I replied back to Ted, "Of course, you're absolutely right. I'm sorry."

A couple of months later, I was a guest on *The Tonight Show Starring Jimmy Fallon,* and Jimmy and I played a game where he googled my name to have me explain the three biggest headlines about me that summer. I wanted to clear the air with Ted Harbert, and since he used to oversee *The Tonight Show Starring Jimmy Fallon,* I knew he would see it.

So, on TV, Jimmy pulled up some recent news stories. One was a picture I had taken with a man in Mallorca, which I had posted in my stories calling the man my "baby." Several news outlets had taken this to mean I was announcing a new relationship.

I explained to Jimmy that the man in the picture was the bartender who works at the bar near my house in Mallorca. Anyone who serves me drinks for a month straight automatically becomes my "baby." I simply wanted to thank him for his service and for being such a good drinking buddy. "Baby" is not a sexual term, or a boyfriend term—it is solely reserved for people who bring me drinks. My publicist reached out asking me to clarify it all on my Instagram, because news outlets were calling to see if I had taken a new lover. Poor baby. A quiet, innocent bartender from Mallorca was now in the *Daily Mail* for being my new man. After I cleared that up, Jimmy went on to read the next headline, CHELSEA HANDLER LEAVES BOYFRIEND TED HARBERT FOR MASSEUSE.

I took this opportunity to retell the part of the story where I was walking downtown and got an email from Ted, and then having to google myself to find out what I did, and being just as shocked as the next person when I saw the headline. *What was I thinking?*

"I'm glad that you brought that up," I told Jimmy. "Because I would like to clarify something. I did not break up with Ted Harbert to be with the masseuse."

"Well," Jimmy said. "I'm not sure that was the part that he was upset about."

"He shouldn't be upset about anything. Do you know how many people have told me they had no idea Ted Harbert was such a stud? I feel like I put him on the map, sexually."

Jimmy agreed that he hadn't ever thought of Ted Harbert as any sort of sexual dynamo and that I definitely had given him some street cred.

"So, you're . . . are you doubling down now?" Jimmy asked, incredulous.

"Yes," I replied. "Ted Harbert and I had a lot of threesomes, but that is not why we broke up."

The first email I saw the next morning was from Ted.

"Uhhh . . . thank you?" he wrote.

"I got your back, buddy," I replied. "Always."

Some habits die hard. Some never die at all.

Drugs aren't for everyone.
However, they are for me and whoever else
is around me that wants what I have.

Mallorca Is
the Tits

visited Mallorca for the very first time for a friend's fortieth birthday. I went with a group of about twenty people. Spending my
childhood summers on Martha's Vineyard naively led me to believe that all islands were small, mostly flat pieces of land.

Mallorca is the opposite. It is mountainous, dramatic, and the size
of a small country. We rented Vespas and rode for hours through
orchards and vineyards, down switchback roads to secluded beach
coves, and then ended the day drinking bottles of white wine while
looking out at the sea. Our hotel sat in the mouth of a harbor that had
two lighthouses on either side, which then opened to the Mediterranean. A view filled with hope and possibility. Boats, a harbor, and the
sound of waves crashing is where I do all my daydreaming.

I took a walk down to the lighthouse one morning and saw a
SE VENDE sign outside what looked like a dilapidated seaside villa.
So, I broke in, and checked out the house to figure out how a property with that kind of view could not have already been scooped up. I
got up to the terrace and looked out at the view from the house.

Smack-dab in the middle of the harbor, and a view I could never tire of. I remember standing on that balcony, looking at my friend Sophie, and saying, "This view is the tits."

I knew then that I needed to buy it. It would be a gift to myself for doing seven years of a talk show, writing three books, and doing three stand-up tours all at the same time. *You've earned this. Get that view to be a permanent one in your life, sister. Think of all the people you can bring here to heal.*

My business managers told me it would be a terrible investment and that the Spanish dollar was weak. I thanked them for their advice and purchased that property, then renovated it in a year. The contractor and designer were excellent, and when they were done, they told me they had an extra thirty-five thousand euros left in my account.

"Keep it," I told them. "As a tip for your honesty."

I knew then the house would be a good omen, blessed with good vibrations.

Each year, I spend a month at my house in Mallorca and invite different groups of friends to come each week. Since I have vastly different friend groups, some come to bike and hike and swim and eat, some come to party, and some come to explore the island and go shopping. Each of my friend groups is into different things, and whatever they're into, I'm into for that week. Unless it's shopping. I prefer never to shop.

As I've made clear, I enjoy supplying people with the right types of drugs to enhance an already magical setting. What you think can't get any more glorious can—with microdosing. Microdosing and Mallorca are the only two tools you need to have a meaningful intervention. Not a drug, alcohol, or sex intervention. A life intervention. When surrounded by that kind of beauty, defenses come down and people are able to heal, hear, and harness their innermost Buddha to change something in their life that isn't working. Add a little LSD to the mix, and people can have life-transforming experiences.

> August 29: Landed this morning, went for a twenty-mile bike ride, came back, and felt a bit off. Took a COVID test. I have COVID.

> August 30: Sitting inside my house in Mallorca, looking out the window at the great blue Mediterranean. Need to let my guests coming know I have COVID. Writing my new book. Womanhood.

> August 31: Am grateful to have COVID in Mallorca. Can't think of a better place to be sick.

> September 1: None of my guests care that I have COVID, and they are all still coming.

The first week I hosted a group of comedians, heavy on the lesbian contingency. A few people in the group had never even been swimming. When I offered up one of the nonswimmers a late-night ride in the kayak, she told me that water sports at night were activities reserved only for white people. She said that white people couldn't be trusted around black people near bodies of water. I finally persuaded her to strap on a life jacket and trust my kayaking skills, and pointed out that we were in a harbor that would prevent us from going more than five miles per hour. After a short deliberation, she tentatively climbed in the kayak at the beach.

I noticed how rigid my friend's arms were holding on to either side of the kayak as I paddled out among the boats. Once we got far enough out, I turned us around so we could look back at the port with all its lights—my house glowing up among them. She gazed up at the star-filled sky and breathed a little. I pointed out Orion's Belt (only because someone had shown it to me a few days before), and then I pointed to other groups of stars and said the names of constellations I remembered from summer nights on Martha's Vineyard. They had to be up there somewhere. After reading about Elon Musk's Starlink, and all the fake stars that are now in the sky, I gave up trying to understand the rest of it, because who really cares if half the stars we are looking at are fake?

My friend and I started talking and it wasn't long before she told me about her mother dying. I stopped paddling and let the kayak idle in the bay. And then she told me more, about her mom's health issues, and her own health issues, and she cried, and then I cried, too. And then we paddled right back to shore. After that I started kayak counseling sessions at midnight. Each night, I'd take a different guest out alone and glide underneath the stars to the different points of the harbor and pull up to the yacht club or to another boat to say hi to anyone we heard on their boats. Most nights, the person would reveal something private about themselves, and it wasn't due to my probing. It was the natural effect of the sea, the midnight blue sky lit up with all the constellations, and the tranquility of being on the water. It softened people and made them contemplate their lives. There is a magic to Mallorca that compels people to take stock, and something in the air provides them with the ease necessary to talk about the things that weigh on them the most but talk about the least.

I had been doing this on my podcast, *Dear Chelsea,* for a couple of years: listening to people's problems, their fears, their disappointments, and then doling out ways for them to make their lives better, pushing people into taking the jump they're scared to take. Here in Mallorca, on the water late at night, I only listened. I understood now the difference between helping and listening. There are times and places for advice, and then there are times where all people need is for someone to listen.

. . .

The next group that came was from Whistler, and with that group there is a lot of exercise. The week consists of daily three-to-eight-hour bike rides around the island. My friend Ange is the ringer in this group and she is always planning long, hard bike rides up and down the coast, because she is always training for a marathon, an Ironman, or something along those lines. Why the rest of us also need to train for whatever event she is training for is lost on me. We all rent electric bikes for the week, because the bike rides are hard, long, and mountainous, and Ange is the only one who does these rides on a regular road bike, because something is very wrong with her. I usually opt out of the longer rides, because the one time I went with them, we left my house at nine in the morning and returned at seven thirty that night. By the time we got home, no one was speaking. Ange had yelled at our friend Isabel for not following directions, each of us had lost gallons of water weight, and everyone was pissed. I informed the group that I would be skipping dinner, and then I passed out from what could only have been heatstroke. I woke up fourteen hours later.

The next morning, the group diagnosed Ange. We were unsure which affliction that she wasn't taking medication for was affecting her the most. Over several liters of red sangria, we decided she had borderline personality disorder, narcissism, ADHD, bipolar disorder, anorexia nervosa, schizophrenia, ADD, sociopathy, and multiple personalities thrown in for good measure.

She has been reading about each disorder ever since.

Now, when those longer bike rides are planned, I spend the day frolicking around my house, or at the beach, working, reading, or taking LSD and sitting around like a zombie staring at the Mediterranean.

. . .

The following week, I hosted a group of eight girls from L.A. in honor of my friend's birthday. We still went on bike rides, but much more reasonable ones. We also went into town a lot, and there was lots of drinking, partying, and cigarettes. I hadn't smoked cigarettes in years after being hypnotized for it in my early forties. The girls who were smoking claimed they only smoked on vacation, plus we were in Europe, so who cares, because you can't get cancer in Europe. Whatever the logic, I joined the party and smoked all week long. We laughed our asses off, and had some very deep heart-to-hearts about different relationships in our lives. On one of my late-night kayak sessions, my friend confided in me about her fraught relationship with her mother. How she hadn't been able to forgive her mother for being so cold and emotionally unavailable, and that she still held so much anger about her. When she broached her childhood and its difficulties with her mom, her mom would get upset and say, "Why bring up the past?"

My friend now had five kids of her own, and was the complete opposite of her own mother. Her kids wouldn't be able to survive without my friend. She is a stellar mom, wife, parent, friend, everything. An all-around A-plus of a person. I let her talk and I listened, because I have also learned that any advice is best served up in the daylight.

The next day out on my terrace, I circled back to our conversation on the kayak. I told my friend that without such a shitty example of a mother she would have never become the mother she is today. That she owed her mother a thank-you for her own good parenting. That her mother showed her what not to do, thereby setting her up for success.

"I'm sure you can find some gratitude in there for her."

"Well, I mean . . . that seems like a stretch," she said.

"No, it only sounds like you are stuck in your anger. You allowing your anger to drive you is toxic. She is the reason you have five beautiful children who love and adore you. If you can let go of your anger, and tell her you forgive her, the tide will rise even higher than it is now. You will have taken the highest road possible, and even more love and compassion will be headed your way, maybe even coming from your mother. Forgiveness is the key to joyful living."

Our other friend Kate was sitting on the terrace with us. "Where do you come up with this shit, Chels?"

"I don't know," I told them. "But I'm very passionate about families making peace and working to get along. No one's family is an accident. There are lessons in everything, and if you fail the course, you have to go to summer school. That's how I look at everything now. I don't want to learn any lesson twice, and I don't want to go to summer school. I want to go to Mallorca."

My friend left Mallorca and sent me a text on my birthday, months later:

> Chelsea, Your wise words regarding my mother made me reflect over the next few weeks and all the anger and resentment melted away for me, internally. I was left with an amazing sense of peace. I reconciled with my mother and was left with appreciation for her and for all that she gave me—the good and the bad. My mom was diagnosed with lung cancer on December 21st. My sister, daughter, and I were able to take care of her 24/7 with the exception of a few hospital stays. She passed away this morning, on your birthday. I wanted to say thank you for caring enough to listen and then pushing me toward forgiveness. She passed away with eight of us surrounding her bed, sending her off with an immense amount of love and honor.

My last group of girlfriends to visit that summer was a group of British girls I had known for years and some of their friends I was meeting for the first time. One of my friends wasn't happy in her career choice—she was being tugged by other possibilities, longings, and family responsibilities. Toward the end of the week, after everyone's roadblocks had been discussed among the rest of the group, we had a sailing day planned, so I grabbed my sheet of LSD.

LSD is a great tool in having deep and meaningful conversations, because it is a heart and love opener, and the sky and the sea and the sand all start to glisten a little more and you start to notice twinkles in people's eyes that you hadn't noticed before.

Once on the boat, I discussed with the group the importance of addressing our concerns with our friend, and that there was no better environment for having an open, honest, loving conversation than on a boat in Mallorca. After all, true friends say things that are hard to say. Especially when they are on LSD. My British friends are very British, slightly emotionally repressed, and were very skittish about having such direct conversations.

"Can I just go in the ocean for another dip before we do it?" one of the women asked me.

"No," I told her. "We're doing it now. I'll do it."

I called our friend over to the bow of the boat and we told her we were going to have a chat. We talked about how special she is and how she seemed to be working so hard for all the wrong reasons, and none that were providing the type of fulfillment she deserved. We reminded her how much she does for everyone else at the expense of her own personal happiness, and that sidelining her own happiness for others is a recipe for regret and resentment. Our friend needed to focus on herself and find her passion and go after it like this is the only life we get.

That day on the boat, I saw a look come over her face, she seemed lit up, the look one gets when they are finally being seen. Being noticed. Hearing people she loved and trusted give it to her straight. After all, she hadn't done anything wrong. She was only guilty of not fulfilling her full potential. She thanked us, and she cried. She needed to hear it, and she went home from that trip, quit her job, and started writing a book she had been contemplating writing for the previous five years.

. . .

Two of my cousins have been married at my house in Mallorca, and many people I have never met have rented it for their own weddings. Many friends of mine have honeymooned there, and my whole family and extended family have spent time there. I've met people who have stayed at my house without me. I share it with every group of friends I have, with my friends' parents, and even with people I've never met. This house isn't just a house; it's a spiritual retreat. Every time someone leaves there, they find themselves filled up with something new.

A friend of mine who came to Mallorca left there promising she was going to publish a children's book she had imagined writing while on safari in Africa. She had seen a young elephant without a tail that inspired her to think of a parable that would appeal to young children who felt like underdogs or outsiders. We encouraged her all week and made her commit to following through and getting this book out. I'm very proud to report that her book was recently published in the U.K., and it is called *The Legend of the Tailless Prince*.

This past September, on my last night on Mallorca, I was next door to my house having goodbye drinks with some friends and some of the locals I had gotten to know and of course Baby. We were sitting outside the bar when I saw an older-looking couple walking past us. They were very adorable and affectionate with each other, linked arm in arm, with the husband also using both his hands to hold his wife's. I smiled at them.

"It's our anniversary," the woman said, smiling back at me. I got up and started walking with them.

"How many years?" I asked.

"Fifty," the man declared pridefully.

"These are my kayaks," I said, pointing toward my kayaks that I had been leaving on the beach after my midnight strolls in the harbor.

"Please take them for a ride. Actually"—I grabbed my LSD out of my pocket—"I have something very special and it is the perfect way for you to spend your fiftieth wedding anniversary."

"What is it?" they asked.

I handed them the LSD and encouraged them to take it, after I made sure neither of them had any heart issues. I sold them on the benefits and assured them it was too mild to be dangerous, and that it would be a night they would never forget.

"Sounds good," said the woman.

"Sure does," said her husband. "I'll have what she's having."

They both ate a microdose of LSD, and opted for one kayak to share instead of two.

When I returned to my friends at the bar, they asked me what I was up to. I explained that I could tell from this couple's affection and demeanor toward each other that they would be great candidates for LSD. If you're already happy, you're only going to get happier.

"How many people do you think you have drugged in this port?" my friend asked me.

"As many people as I can," I said. "Don't you want the world to be a happier place?"

I am an interloper. I interlope because nine times out of ten, real friends can and do make a difference. Not all my interloping ends well. Sometimes, people are so stuck they can't see the forest for the trees, and they can't see their way out of it, and no matter how much help and support you provide, they are unable to be pulled up. This is incredibly frustrating and hard to watch, but it also has been an exercise in letting go. Letting go of situations that you may not be able to improve, letting go of the expectation that people want their lives to be different. Sometimes, it's more comfortable for people to sit in the muck they are familiar with, because the unknown is scarier. There have been people who are not interested in my interloping. I understand how strong I can come across, but my intent is to share my strength, not to diminish anyone else's.

The couple in their seventies resurfaced at seven the next morning. I was up and doing a workout on my balcony, when I spotted them kayaking up to the beach and placing my kayak in the sand.

"Are you guys just getting back?" I asked.

"Yes!" the woman shouted up to my terrace. They had spent the night in a cave around the corner out on the coastline up toward Sa Calobra. They clambered up the steps to my terrace and I opened the gate. The man took my face in his hands, and told me that I had made their night.

"We thought we were having a good time, but apparently we didn't know what a good time was."

Then the woman looked at me and asked, "Do you have any more of that LSD?"

September 30: I am out of LSD.

360 Review

One year, a close friend of mine joined me and my family on our summer excursion to Martha's Vineyard. This trip was a little different because we were missing some core family members who either were dropping off kids at college or were the kids being dropped off at college. In their absence, I invited some of my California cousins with their partners and two of their three-year-old babies.

It was a great infusion of energy having babies around, and also having my cousins, who were so grateful to be included in our vacation and who constantly chipped in with cooking and helping around the house to show their appreciation.

We were sitting outside having dinner one night when I mentioned how nice it was to have some younger people on vacation with us, instead of just the usual brothers, sisters, nieces, nephews, and husbands and wives of my siblings.

My friend who was visiting is a career CEO of one company or another and was telling us about a recent 360 review she had experienced, where each of her direct reports critiqued her performance as their boss and relayed back to her what her strengths and weaknesses as a CEO were. Talk about empowering employees and keeping CEOs in check.

"I like that idea!" I exclaimed. Being the CEO of my family, I thought a feedback loop and a performance review on vacation could be very eye-opening for all of us. Who contributes? Who only takes? Who cooks, cleans, makes drinks? What is everyone's value proposition?

"Let's do an anonymous 360!" I exclaimed. "We can all review each other!"

"Giving performance reviews to family members?" my sister Shana replied. "That sounds more like a non-anonymous 360. I don't think this seems like a good idea."

"Only if you're not contributing," I said.

"I like this idea, too," my brother Roy chimed in, excitedly. "I feel like it could displace a lot of family members."

"Well," I said, admiring the company of my cousins and their cheerful dispositions, "it seems like sprinkling some new blood into the mix has had a positive impact on everyone here, no?"

"We're not doing anonymous or non-anonymous 360s, Chelsea," Simone said. "This isn't *Survivor*. It's a family vacation."

"That's what makes a non-monogamous 360 so exciting! Who will survive and who won't?" Roy added.

"It's non-*anonymous*," Shana jumped in, correcting Roy.

"It's actually supposed to be just 'anonymous,'" my CEO friend added. "You're not supposed to know who the review is coming from."

"But we will know," Shana said. "We'll all know exactly who it came from. As if we are not all going to recognize Chelsea's review?"

"But why am I being forced to go on vacation with all of your partners and children every year?" I asked. "It doesn't seem fair that because of your life decisions, my life has to be impacted. You are the people who got married, and now I'm married to these people? I have lots of people I'd like to add to these trips and a few I wouldn't mind subtracting. I mean, it has been twenty-five years of vacations with your spouses. Is that really what God had in store for me?"

"Here we go," Simone moaned, moving to the pool and lying down on a chaise.

We all followed her over there.

"I'm just saying, I feel like we can all do a little bit better on family vacations, knowing that we are not all here on vacation alone, but that we are with a large group and we should consider that while making personal plans and activities. Is everyone here doing their best? I'm not sure . . ."

"And, who is going to review you?" Shana asked.

"The Lord," Glen chimed in, sarcastically. "The same person who is going to review all of us."

"Anyone who wants to," I told Shana confidently, ignoring Glen. "I have nothing to hide. However, I do believe there are a couple of family members who could use a little encouragement. I don't really think they're delivering much in a vacation setting."

"We know!" Simone, Shana, and Roy said in unison. "Everyone knows!"

While it is not necessary to always keep my family on high alert with threats of excommunication, for certain members it is fun to share new ideas. I enjoyed watching everyone's reactions to the possibility of a 360 anonymous non-monogamous review.

While I am not pursuing a formal performance appraisal of each family member, it is good practice to evaluate people's place in your life. It is good to encourage people to think harder about what their added value is, to assess it, and to know that there is always room for improvement from everyone—including myself.

"Remember the letter you sent us where you told us all how we needed to step it up?" Simone asked.

"Ahhh, yes. I remember it like it was yesterday," Glen said, fondly.

"Well, apparently that letter has been going around, because one of my friends from law school sent it to me and said, 'This is a great letter to send to all families.' She thought I might like to send it to my own. I didn't want to tell her that I was one of the letter's original recipients."

"What a full-circle moment," I said, smiling. I loved hearing that the letter had been making the rounds. I, too, had a friend of mine send me my own letter, not knowing I was its original author. Apparently, I had shared the letter with my agent, and then it took on a life of its own.

"Speaking of your areas for self-improvement," Simone added. "It would be nice for us to have a family vacation without being threatened about not being invited on one again."

"But then how would I spend my time?" I asked her, sipping on my margarita.

Allée of Trees

was breaking up with a boyfriend and I wanted to give him a parting gift—something that would remind him of me and also something he wouldn't be able to get rid of.

So, I imported thirty-five linden trees from Germany to line either side of his driveway. The trees met overhead to form a canopy over the long entryway to his country estate.

This was an extravagant gift, and I wanted the gesture to be extravagant because that's how I felt at the time. I knew the relationship was unhealthy and I was finally ready to make a break. What helped me part ways was knowing that every spring and fall, the leaves on the linden trees would change color, and everyone who came to his house would comment on them, and then, in turn, he would be reminded of what he'd lost.

And now, every spring and fall, I get a picture from him with a text saying, "Thank you, Yelsi, Your trees are changing color. It's time to come home."

He and I both know I'll never see those trees again, but I think fondly of those trees as one of my best gifts of all time.

Nothing stands the test of time quite like a tree. Leaves come and go. Always be the tree.

There have been many times in my life
where I have confused success with
getting what I want, rather than knowing that
success is giving. It is never only about you.
That's where it starts, of course, but
as we grow and evolve, it can and should
be about what you are able to give others.
Not in the material sense, but in the
spiritual sense. Whom can you show up
for, and how far are you willing to go
for others? How much love do you have
to give . . . and are you sure that's all?

Doug Handler

This past winter, after a month in Whistler, I headed back to Los Angeles for four days to host the Critics Choice Awards. I had been asked to host the show for the second time in a row, and it was a fun gig the year before. I knew I would be able to replicate that night for everyone. It's very hard for me to leave my little Whistler village in winter, but I had been working consciously to appreciate the commitments I make without complaining about them. I began looking forward to all my obligations and worked at remaining in the grounded feeling I had learned to lean into and plant myself in. The feeling of being the tree that withstands wind and storms, that remains grounded no matter what the outside noise betrays. To remain rooted in who I am, and not let silly stuff throw me off my game.

My new house in L.A. was still under construction and was two and a half years late, so I thought it was high time I moved my ass in there to let my contractor, designer, and all the workmen know that they needed to fucking step on it.

Only my bedroom, bathroom, and gym were ready, so they set it up like a hotel suite, since that's where I spend most of my time anyway. The first night there, my assistants let me know that once I was secure in my room, they would set the alarm and it would disable at five thirty the next morning.

"Can I open my terrace door?" I asked Mabel. "In case it gets too hot?"

"No, the alarm isn't yet set up for bypassing. That's tomorrow. Once you're in, just stay in. Text us if you need to get out of the house before 5:30 a.m. and we'll disarm the alarm."

"Thanks?" Then she kissed me good night and tucked me into bed like an eight-year-old.

So, I spent the first night at my new house that was basically a hotel room within a construction site trapped in a tower like Rapunzel, sweating my balls off because the thermostat was set to seventy-five degrees. Years earlier, not having the thermostat at my preferred temperature of sixty-eight would have resulted in me being pissed, but nothing that inconsequential was going to ruin my mood. I was home to be hosting an awards show, and that was my main focus.

Among other discomforts, it didn't feel right to be in a home of my own without a dog's company, so I texted my assistant to ask if we had made any headway finding Bernice a new big brother. Once I had cemented my relationship with Bernice, I put out the feelers that I was looking for a new rescue to complete our family. Nothing like finally getting Bernice where I wanted her and then destabilizing the relationship with a new addition to the family.

There were two chow chows available from the same rescue where I got Bert and Bernice, and the rescue people were driving down to showcase these two dogs at a dog park in Brentwood.

As mentioned earlier, I've had some of my worst interactions with people at dog parks. This interaction was a particular highlight.

I walked into the Brentwood dog park that had two metal gates leading in, and left both gates slightly open, because I stood no more than five feet away looking to see if there was a group of chow chows anywhere.

"Excuse me, close the fucking gates please!" a man walking toward me shouted.

"I'm looking for a dog," I told him.

"It takes one second before one of these dogs runs out of the park and gets hit by a car on Barrington," he wailed.

I looked in his direction to make sure I was getting the full picture of this hysteria. He was walking hastily toward me with two small dogs on leashes. There were no other dogs or people nearby.

"No one is getting hit by a car, and please stop screaming at me," I implored.

I looked at my phone, trying to ascertain from the pin drop if I was in the right place. This was when I noted I was dealing with a gay man. As if I hadn't spent the last twenty-five years making my allyship clear. I would expect this behavior from a straight man, maybe. But, to their credit, straight men don't typically run through dog parks screaming at strangers.

"You celebrities are so entitled; you think you can just walk into dog parks and do whatever you want," he wailed, as he came closer. On behalf of celebrities everywhere, I took great offense at this comment.

"Um, sir? Obviously, something happened to you this morning, because you are screaming at a stranger, and I'm pretty sure this has nothing to do with me. I'm looking for a dog."

"Ha! Looking for a dog? Because you lost them?"

"No, I didn't lose a dog. Sir, will you please stop talking to me?" I had one eye on the guy I was dealing with and one eye on my phone, trying to figure out where I was supposed to be, because logistics are not my métier.

"You're a whore, Chelsea Handler!" was his next comment.

To this, it was impossible not to laugh.

"Whoa," said a stranger from behind. I turned to see a man walking toward us with his pit bull. "Pretty toxic doggy park, huh?" he asked, eyes wide from hearing me being called a whore. "You need any help here?"

"No, I'm good," I told him. "Just dealing with an angry gay." By this point, the gay man had deposited himself inside his minivan with his windows closed, snapping pictures of me. I made sure to look up, smile, and wave.

This was when I realized I was at the wrong dog park. I was supposed to be across the street. I guess the universe wanted to make sure I was called a whore that day.

I drove across the street to the right dog park and spotted the rescue people and two dogs. One was a blue chow, which is actually gray, and the other was jet black. It was obvious which one would be mine from the car. I knew my next dog would have to be of color. Doug was a giant black eight-month-old full chow chow. I have only dreamed of having a full chow chow because rescues typically only have chow mixes, and here was a full chow, whose very full body was just about to bloom, who had already been housebroken, and who was a complete and absolute home run.

I took Doug straight home to my little tree house and patted my bed, and he jumped right up. After twenty years of rescuing dogs, I realized that my dog karma had finally caught up to me, and I was looking at the man of my dreams. And, he didn't lick me. He has his perfect black chow tongue and never licks anyone. I've never appreciated getting licked by a dog, a person, or even Whoopsie and Oopsie, who liked to lick me when they needed to wake me up.

Doug was next-level. All of my dogs have been lovable, chunky, or affectionate, but not all in one dog. I had to get different things from different dogs, but now I had my dream dog. He's black, full-bodied, and affectionate with everyone and can run. I hadn't had a dog who ran since Chunk. I forgot that real dogs run, and that most dogs typically like to play with other dogs and be social. That's Doug. He runs up to everyone and loves on everyone. He is not discerning about whom he mingles with. Bernice doesn't give anyone the time of day.

Doug is a social butterfly. It felt as if I had designed my very own dream dog and my order had finally been filled by Santa Claus himself.

The next day was rehearsal and writers' meetings for the Critics Choice Awards. I knew that if I brought my highest vibes and energy I would set the tone for an evening of fun and celebration—and that's just what I did. Even though my formal therapy had ended years before, I was still getting better at knowing how to remain positive, optimistic, and upbeat, and not letting silly things, like sleeping in seventy-five-degree heat or being called a whore, dampen my mood. I was reclaiming the groundedness that I had lost during my Netflix show. It wasn't something that happened overnight, and it took time, work, meditation, reflection, and then what was once a fleeting feeling started happening more frequently.

The nervous energy I used to have seemed to disappear and I felt centered, clear, and focused in all my career endeavors. I knew that my attitude was the key ingredient to this turnaround. No more victim mentality when things weren't working or if I wasn't getting offers that excited me. No more laying the blame at my agent's feet for not procuring me more stuff. I stopped all that whining and complaining and became grateful. I became grateful and positive and thanked people all the time for any opportunities that came my way, whether they were of interest to me or not. I looked at my stand-up shows with excitement and appreciation no matter where I was performing. I decided to change everything about the way I approached life, and rather than have ups and downs, I was going to be constant. Constantly grateful, and I was going to start showing anyone who doubted me that I was never to be doubted.

During rehearsal, I looked around and saw all the cardboard cutouts of the celebrities who'd be in attendance. De Niro, DiCaprio, Scorsese, Oprah.

Oprah had interviewed me years earlier, at the height of my success on *Chelsea Lately*. When her crew arrived at my house to set up, everyone seemed very nervous. Was Oprah going to walk up my driveway or would she want a golf cart? Would she want to film her entrance? I wasn't nervous. I always expected to be interviewed by Oprah. I believed that about myself, perhaps a little too much at the time. It was a period in my life when no one blew me away or impressed me. The Critics Choice Awards was my opportunity to make a new impression. I was vibing high, and my intention was to take everyone, including Oprah, with me.

I recognized the way I felt the day of the show, and noted that I had never felt more confident about how well I would do. I was devoid of butterflies or nerves, which I had learned to accept as a signal that I cared about whatever I was going to do. This was another level of confidence I was experiencing, a newer version of capability. I knew I would go out on that stage and show everyone what an excellent host looks like, without having to make anyone feel bad, or humiliate anyone. To show grace, and humor, and to be a fucking boss.

I was prepared and patient, and any stress of that day had absolutely no impact on me. I couldn't wait to get out on that stage. I have had so many high-profile or high-stakes moments in my career, and I have never felt so solid as I did on that day. I had been feeling it on tour each night for almost two years. My confidence had gone from shaken when I started doing stand-up again, to the fullest, most competent I had ever felt. I was finally here, in my own shoes. The woman I wanted to become was standing with me, in me. All of my hard work, all of my therapy, all of my learning and understanding that the negative unkind voice or shadow self we have is not who we really are. The essence of who we are is the best version of ourselves, and my essence is ebullient. I choose light. Here I am. Here she is. Here we are.

. . .

I went backstage after my opening ten-minute monologue and walked right into Oprah's outstretched arms. She told me how great of a host I was and that I should be hosting all award shows. It was praise heaped on me by one of the people I respect the most, and it felt as if heaven itself was wrapping me up and telling me "good job." I had made a new impression. A better one. I had shown the person in that room whom I cared about most that when I knew better, I did better.

I had Oprah's approval and I had Doug. And, I had my own approval. *You did this, and made it look easy,* I told myself at the end of the show. I slept like a baby that night. I returned to Whistler on the first flight out the next day. I needed to get back to my happy place, because something was tugging at me. Sometimes the universe is telling you to sit down and read a book. This time it was telling me to sit down and write one. *I have something new to say,* I thought.

When I arrived in Vancouver, I was picked up by a driver for my two-hour ride back to Whistler.

When we were thirty minutes outside Squamish, I was unable to ignore the need to urinate. I told my driver it would be in his best interest to find a place to stop, any place, but he said there really wasn't any place to stop except on the side of the icy Sea-to-Sky Highway, which doesn't really have a shoulder. While holding my crotch and vigorously shifting my vaginal weight back and forth over my jeans, I made it all the way to my house. But when I stepped outside the vehicle, my bladder gave out. I stood on the side of the driveway, holding Doug on a leash, staring at the driver, and peeing right through my jeans, feeling my shoes fill with urine and then overflow into puddles on the concrete. I ran in my squishy jeans and urine-soaked sneakers right to my front door, and disrobed on my way to the laundry room.

Well, I guess last night is officially over. That didn't take long. Any-

time I have become too pleased with myself, the universe steps in to re-mind me of my humanness.

Soon after I returned to Whistler, Ange was eager to film my birthday video and get it out of the way. She had filmed my last four birthday videos, and because of all of the logistics required, we wanted to get it over with. We decided with the new addition to my family, for my forty-ninth birthday video we would put Bernice on my back in a BabyBjörn, and Doug would run behind us down the hill. Doug wasn't as cooperative as we had hoped. He was confused and didn't know which way to run, and we had a lot of different people yelling different directions at him. This was Doug's first foray into on-camera work, as well as his first time on the slopes, and it wasn't a seamless production. So, we got the birthday video, but Ange and I both knew we could do better.

"I think we need to get a shot of you skiing holding Doug in your arms," Ange said later that afternoon when we were looking through the footage. "He's too good-looking not to get a close-up of him. I know the shot I want."

I had already lost interest in getting back into a bikini and heading back on the mountain. Between the dogs, wearing a bikini, holding a joint in one hand and a margarita in the other, the whole fiasco just attracts too much attention. People stop, they want to start taking pictures, and it's hard to wrangle strangers who never agreed to be in a shoot in the first place.

"Ugh, again? It's such a process filming these videos; I think it will be fine with Doug just running behind me."

Ange was intent. "We we we we just need to get the shot of you ski-ing down the mountain with Doug in your arms," she repeated. "It it it it's going to make the whole video." When Ange is excited, she doesn't start or finish sentences, she just picks up in the middle of a sentence and starts stuttering until she can weave her thoughts together.

"Okay, okay," I said with a sigh, knowing she was right—having a close-up of Doug and his beauty would make a better video. He is just so handsome he takes people's breath away.

So, we did it all again.

I changed back into my bikini, strapped Bernice in her backpack, and got my ski stuff together. We charged out to the closest part of the mountain, and I hiked up the ski hill with my skis on my shoulders, Bernice on my back with her ski goggles on, and Doug on a leash. We climbed up for about fifty yards, and when we got to the top, I put my skis on. As I was holding Bernice in the backpack and holding Doug with both hands about to try to ski a few turns, Ange yells to me, "What about the joint and margarita?"

"How would you like me to hold them, Ange?" I snapped back, as if she was some director who had hired me for a shoot. Doug was sixty-five pounds at this point, and Bernice was thirty, and with all the adrenaline I felt like I was going to have a heart attack.

"Oh, right," she realized, seeing I had no free hands to hold anything.

"Okay, I'm going to start. Ready?"

"Wait!" she yelled.

"I can't!" I screamed back. "I'm going!"

"Ski!" she yelled, and then, "Turn!"

I started coming down the mountain, but couldn't actually turn my skis holding so much weight, so I ended up just snowplowing down the mountain with Doug in my arms.

"Do it!" Ange yelled. "Turn!"

"I can't fucking turn! He's too heavy!" I snowplowed to a stop and put Doug down. I was starting to feel the back of my hair get moist—which is not a word I like to throw around.

"I think you need to just turn twice," she said, while I was catching my breath. "Just one more time! I'll get the shot. I promise!" So, I hiked back up the fifty yards, this time with Doug in my arms. I knew if I could get up the mountain with him in my arms, coming down would seem like a breeze, and then maybe I could turn, and that's just what happened. I made about four turns with Doug in my arms and then skied right up to Ange and put Doug down in front of her so we could get our close-up.

Then we walked back to my house and went upstairs, where I grabbed a protein bar and a can of Moscow mule and sat down at my kitchen counter, in a bikini covered in sweat.

"Thanks, Ange. I really wasn't in the mood to do that again."

"Is that your dinner?" she asked me, disgusted. Ange knows first-hand that the only cooked meals I get are at her house or out at a restaurant, and that it's best that I just don't try to cook anything.

So, she rifled through my fridge, took out some frozen chicken from the freezer and a bunch of other random things, some spices—probably left over from the previous owner four years earlier—and whipped up one of the best chicken dishes I've ever had. She did this all in her tank top with her little tiny body and huge muscles, because she, too, was hot from running up and down the ski hill. Then she made two plates of it, and we sat down at my dinner table and ate. Afterward, she put the leftover chicken in Tupperware containers.

"There, that should last a week. You can't eat protein bars for dinner. You're about to be forty-nine."

An hour or two later, we were sitting in my living room hanging out talking, when Ange hastily got up.

"Okay, okay, I'm leaving," Ange said, as if I had asked her to leave three times already. "I saw the look."

"What look?"

"The look that says you are done with everyone for the night."

"But you're the only one here," I told her.

"Yeah, and I just got the look, so I'll see you tomorrow."

She got me to do something I wasn't in the mood for; then she made me dinner and then left when she knew I wanted to be alone. This is the definition of a sister.

After a few weeks of having Doug at home, Bernice started running again. She would play with him in the mornings and grab for the toys in his mouth. They'd pull back and forth from each other, but Doug could tell Bernice was much weaker than him, so he would tug lightly in order to humor her. It was adorable. When Doug would try to come up on my bed in Whistler, Bernice would stand on her haunches and let him know to back the fuck off. Bernice is alpha, and Doug is type B. I'm a little of both. I'm type A in the morning until I get all my shit done at about noon, and then I turn into type Z. I had a new neurodiverse family, and I was ready for all that came with it.

Having to work with Doug on his commands and recall became a daily two-hour job, with me and my fanny pack filled with dog treats. By the end of winter, I had dog treats in every ski jacket pocket and drawer in my house. I even had them in the shower, because Doug was always trying to see me naked. Where I used to find edibles, mushrooms, or some laced chocolate, there was now a steady supply of salmon treats. I smelled like salmon the entire winter, and I can officially say that parenting classes are a lot more interesting than dog training classes.

My first dog trainer for Doug asked what I was looking to get out of his training. She informed me that our first session would be a "discovery" session.

When I looked at her with a blank stare, she offered up some examples of the services she provided.

"And what about shaking a paw?" she asked me. "Rolling over, playing dead?"

"No," I told her. "Those aren't concerns of mine, and quite frankly not a priority at all. I'd like him to come when I call his name? That's a big one. And to not assault people. I'd like to avoid that."

Then one night she sent me links to five different YouTube tutorials about dog recall and a written questionnaire to fill out about me and my dog's personality. I didn't have the heart to tell her that I certainly wouldn't be taking any written exams about my dog.

The dog walker was a separate story. She took multiple dogs on walks each day and was willing to let Doug audition with a big group of dogs to see if he could play well with others.

After his first day, she texted me and reported that he was loving and compassionate. How anyone could tell if a dog was compassionate while on a walk with other dogs was confusing. Was he comforting the other dogs? Was he picking up litter and recycling bottles? How does a dog demonstrate compassion on a walk? By listening carefully to other dogs while they bark? My main attraction to Doug was that he was affectionate without being needy. He was perfectly happy cuddling or playing, *or* doing his own thing. Pretty much what I am looking for in a partner.

Between scheduling Doug's dog walker, dog trainer, and life coach, and sessions with my own new therapist, I had my days full, and a lot less time for skiing. Instead of looking at what I was missing, I doubled down. After all my own work, I had the energy and bandwidth for all of it. I had put enough time into myself, freeing me up to be in a position to focus on others. I even started taking Doug's new friends in our neighborhood for walks with us so that he could play together with other dogs.

The most important thing was keeping him out of Mabel's clutches for long enough for me to imprint on him so that when we went back to L.A., all of Mabel's tricks, briberies, and Spanish weren't going to brainwash him into thinking he was hers. I wasn't going to spend the rest of Doug's life watching Mabel lure him away from me with her body and whatever else she was offering up.

Spring Break

Whoopsie and Oopsie and I had stayed in touch over the years, but after seeing their sister Poopsie in London and bringing her to Mallorca with me, I realized how meaningful it would be to get to spend some real time with them. I checked with their parents, who gave me their blessing to invite the girls to visit me in Whistler.

The two of them arrived for spring break one morning in March. They went through the roof when they met Doug. Talk about a perfect addition to our family.

"Look, Father. Doug is trying to hug me!" Oopsie screamed as they were cuddling on the floor. She was rubbing Doug's belly and Doug had all four paws in the air and looked like he was actually attempting to hug her. I was over the moon. *A dog who can give hugs?* I went over for a hug from Doug, too, and accidentally called him Bert.

"Sorry, Dirk," I said, in an attempt to correct myself.

"Dirk?" Oopsie and Whoopsie laughed.

"Yes, Dirk and Denise. Those will be the dogs' porn names," I told them. Oopsie grabbed the doggy treats and started teaching Doug to give his paw.

"I've never understood why people teach their dogs to give their paw," I said. "What's the point of that?"

"Because it's cute," she informed me.

"Is it, though? I don't find it cute; I find it more of a reflection of the owner. I'd rather use a dog's time more wisely. At this point, shouldn't they be able to do some sort of accounting?"

I went over to Bernice to reassure her that even though I had brought home an interloper, she was and will always be my number one baby.

"Girls, we have to make sure Bernice knows she is the queen and that Bert, Dirk, Doug, or whatever his name is, will need to defer to her. Fuck. Why can't I get his name right?"

"Father, this is the best way to remember. Bert is the past, Bernice is the present, and Doug is the future," Oopsie declared.

Moments later, as I was making a cocktail, I dropped some ice on the kitchen floor. Doug came running over and started chewing on the ice, spitting it out when it got too cold, and then grabbing it again off the floor.

"Father, now we know he is your son!" Whoopsie exclaimed. "He loves ice just as much as you do!"

When the girls were younger, we used to play a game where I would say, "Name a color," and then the three of us would stare back and forth at one another, and on the count of three we would all yell out our answers. Eventually, if we practiced this enough, we could become telepathic, I told them.

"Girls," I said, as we sat down to dinner one night in Whistler. "Think of a color. Don't say it out loud. On the count of three. One, two, three."

"Purple!" we all screamed in unison.

"TV show," I said. "One, two, three."

"*White Lotus*!" they screamed. I screamed, "*Bridgerton*."

"Singer. One, two, three."

"Lana Del Rey!" we yelled, knowing that was always their answer.

"Country," I commanded.

"Paris," said the girls, while I yelled, "Brazil."

"Girls, Paris is not a fucking country!" Their geographical knowledge and spelling were still areas that needed improvement, and it was astonishing.

"Now spell 'Alaska'!"

"A . . l . . . a . . s . . . k . . . a!"

"Yes!"

"Spell 'Hawaii.'" They looked at each other with big eyes. "One, two, three."

"H . . a . . w . . . e . . ."

"No. Think about it and look into each other's eyes."

"H . . A . . W . . A . . I . . I."

I was intent on getting them to get better at spelling, and for their grammar to improve.

I had only recently gotten Whoopsie to stop using the word "anyways." The girls knew that I had certain grammatical triggers, and "anyways" is probably in the top spot. That, and when people say, "these ones." When I hear someone say "these ones" or "anyways," I have a tic that presents as getting the chills. I have to look away in disgust. I don't know why people don't care about grammar or spelling, but I find good spelling and grammar to be an aphrodisiac. When I get a text from a guy I'm interested in, and there is a spelling error, an emoji, or no sentence structure, it is unlikely we will be interacting again. While this may sound harsh, it is my truth and, in my estimation, is a matter of self-respect.

"Now spell 'animal,'" I said. "One, two, three." They stared at each other, eyes locked.

"One, two, three . . ." I counted slowly.

"Hippo Rape!" they shouted. I had been on a safari with my nieces and one of my sisters earlier that year. There, I had learned more than

I could ever want to know about animal penetration. I couldn't wait to tell the girls about the hippo rape I had witnessed alongside the Mara River in Tanzania, so I sent them a picture from Africa of it happening in real time with the caption "Hippo Rape."

During our safari, we pulled up to a tributary off the Mara River where a male hippo was throttling what we assumed was a female hippo, from a forty-five-degree angle, above the water. The female hippo was underwater during the pummeling, and there really was no question as to what was going on.

"Can she breathe?" my niece asked.

"Hippos can breathe for eight minutes underwater," Rex, our guide, explained.

"What if it takes longer than eight minutes?" another niece asked.

"Safari rapes don't usually last eight minutes," I interjected.

"How do you know?" my first niece asked.

"I don't really know, but these are animals, so they're definitely not 'making love.'"

"This is awful," my sister said. "Who wants to get penetrated with your head underwater?"

"Who wants to get penetrated by a fucking hippo?"

"Hippos," our ranger, Peter, told us. "Hippo on hippo."

"Hippo on hippo rape," Simone added.

When that hippo was done, another male hippo jumped up on the female and started pummeling her.

"Oh, no. A gang bang," I said, looking down. "That's disheartening."

"Hippos are not monogamous," Rex said.

"Well, it doesn't seem like the women have any choice, so it's really the men who are non-monogamous."

Earlier that day, we had tracked a female lion in heat who was being pursued by the head lion from their pride. The patriarch follows the female in heat around the bush until she is ready for some action. Then, once he is done with her and believes he has planted his seed, the next dominant lion in the pride comes and has his way with her. So, essentially this is a gang bang as well, but the female lion has to acquiesce, so there is a modicum of dignity in the process. We also learned that female lions can get pregnant by two different lions on the same day. Since all the men in the pride have access to the female in heat, they have a pecking order to follow. But it's common for the female to produce two cubs, each from a different father. We were fascinated by this.

"That sounds like one fucked-up family," Oopsie said now, over dinner.

"Father, it sounds like you should go back over there and fix their family. The way you fixed us," Whoopsie suggested.

"No, I want Father to stay with us," Oopsie said. "Childhood is almost over."

"Father is always with us, even when she's not," Whoopsie said to Oopsie.

That was the single best sentence I've ever heard in my life.

Then Oopsie showed me that she had changed my contact in her phone to "Hippo Rape."

"You cannot have me in your phone as 'Hippo Rape,' honey. That's something that could bite me in the ass down the line."

"Bite you in the ass with your head underwater," Whoopsie said, cracking herself up.

"Fine," Oopsie said. "I'll change it back to 'Father.'"

March 13: Met a very hot mountain man today. He asked me on a date, but I have the girls this week. Therapist told me it is important to make the girls know that they are the priority. Introducing a man to the scenario takes attention from them, and also, they don't need to know anything about my love life. Not appropriate. So, now I'm passing up a new lover for my daughters.

March 14: Girls arrive for spring break.

March 15: I came home from skiing, and the girls weren't even home. Which meant that they had gone to the village together. Which meant they were loving each other, and it makes me so happy when they get along!

March 18: Dinner with the girls. They are getting along so well now it is making my heart so full. So grateful to have my girls. The love is real and it is deep.

March 19: The best thing about the girls is the kindness they bring out in me. They have made me so much more gentle. I love them something fierce.

March 20: Girls are leaving in the morning. Last night, Whoopsie grabbed my hand at dinner and leaned in with her biggest saddest face: "I miss you even when I'm with you."

March 21: Am so grateful for this time with the girls on their spring break with me in Whistler. I love them so much. They are big bundles of challenging joy, and they are making me do things I would not do for any other children. It is good for me. Grateful for this winter of happiness. Have been trying to spread as much joy and laughter as possible.

Ebullience

For a long time, I pondered whether or not I was a *good* person. I had been blaming myself for having very human feelings like jealousy and lustfulness, the wanting of karma to kick in to the people who deserved it. The inability to be happy for someone's success that exceeded my own. That is not what makes you a bad person. Acting on those instincts is what makes you a bad person. But even then, no one is permanently bad. You can correct anytime you want. You can start the day tomorrow and put an end to old or destructive behavior. You can learn to understand that everyone deserves success and happiness, and that it is no threat to you when someone else finds their own, or even exceeds yours.

Meditation is a practice because it takes repetition and time to feel the impact of the effort you put toward it. Like many things in life, it is our choice to decide what type of person we are aiming to become. To be present-minded, be fully aware, and have mental clarity aren't easy things to come by. I know the work I had to put in to get the negative voices out of my head, to look inward when I feel down, to pick up a book and read. That is also a practice.

This is what I imagine when I meditate: Red and orange lights enveloping me. My mother and my brother Chet somewhere above me as miniature versions of themselves, taking the shape of celestial be-ings, like little Greek nymphs dancing through the sky. I use this prac-tice to calm any uneasy feelings, to allow myself to breathe, and to restore and remind myself that this gift I have grown to respect is not only for me, but it is to exercise patience, love, and compassion for everyone I see that day. It is a reset, a focus to demonstrate love and spread joy. To be ebullient. To expand the light around me so that it grows bigger and brighter and is infectious to others. To always choose light.

Won't You Be My Neighbor?

B y the end of the season in Whistler, I had amassed a large following of children. It wasn't just that Oopsie and Whoopsie visited, but other children had become fixtures in my life, too. Between the dogs, the dogs' friends, and all these kids, my life in Whistler had somehow turned into a full-blown day-care center. I'd ski with kids, eat with kids, they'd show up at my house to play with Doug or Bernice, or gather in my upper living room to play video games. They ranged from eight-year-olds to nineteen-year-olds, and I could not shake them.

Some days I'd ski with my friend Jannicke's son Jack, who was nineteen and wanted me to ski off cliffs alongside him. Luckily, due to all of my previous training I was able to shimmy my ass out of these situations at the last possible minute, but I liked the idea of being present for him and giving him the attention he needed while skiing off cliffs and dropping off jumps. (I'm not sure this is the right vernacular for what Jack was doing, but these are my language skills as it relates to skiing.)

Other days, I'd ski with Jack's little brother Calvin, who was a twelve-year-old bundle of joy. Calvin liked to drag me through terrain parks, which meant I would ski ahead and then record him on my phone skiing off jumps and half-pipes—if that's what they're even called.

Calvin and I had endless things to talk about, mostly because Calvin can talk to himself for hours. I enjoyed my time with both of the boys immensely. My maternal or paternal instinct had kicked into full gear, and I felt a sense of responsibility to children everywhere now, after seeing the positive impact it had had on the girls. I was finally grasping the idea that all children are all of our responsibilities. To give them our time and create fun and listen and learn from them.

One afternoon when Calvin and I were skiing, I made a lunch reservation at a bar at one of the nicer restaurants on the mountain, and when I arrived, they looked at Calvin and asked if it was just the two of us.

"It sure is," I said, confidently.

"We can't have minors sitting at the bar, Chelsea," the hostess informed me.

I hadn't considered that, as I go to a restaurant most days on the mountain for a margarita juice boost—whether I'm with friends or skiing alone. So instead of seating us at the bar, the hostess put us at a dining table for two in the middle of the restaurant. Calvin and I sat across from each other, like a couple on a date. I sipped my margarita, while he discussed his love of ice hockey and skiing, and I wondered how I had turned into Mrs. Doubtfire.

My friend Martha has two sons named Charlie and Brooks, ages seventeen and fifteen, and whenever they came up from Squamish to ski, they'd text me to meet up. Between Jack, Calvin, Charlie, and Brooks, I was becoming more and more hopeful for the future of mankind. They were all such great young men. All engaging, all interested and interesting. Polite, with good manners, and confident without being arrogant. I wasn't used to teenage boys who could make conversation with adults. I was so impressed with them, and it was nice hanging out with boys, too. Less drama, more skiing, and a time for me to breathe.

All four boys loved my dogs up and would always offer to take them for a walk or play with them. Sometimes they'd come up for the day, for the night, or sometimes the whole family would move in for the weekend. Calvin and Bernice had a special connection, so Bernice was always in his arms when he was at my house, and when I went out of town, Bernice stayed with Calvin and his mom.

My cousins Molly and Kerry came to visit for a few days with their own two- and three-year-old daughters. "Don't you think it's weird that all these kids are surrounding you when you claim you don't even like them?" Molly asked one day. "It's not even like you have anything to offer them. You have no good snacks at your house or even any real food. All you have are drugs and alcohol and egg whites."

"Don't forget my orange juice. I always have orange juice."

"You're not giving these kids drugs, are you?" Molly delivered this sentence in an accusatory way, as if I would actually give drugs to children.

"No, Molly. I don't have any extra drugs to give them, because I am taking all my drugs in order to deal with this onslaught. Speaking of which, I need you to find my sheet of LSD!" Molly will find anything I have ever lost, because she knows exactly how my brain works when I forget.

I explained to her that due to the number of children meandering through my house that winter, I had hid an entire sheet of acid in my closet drawer, and when I looked for it days later, it was nowhere to be found. Even Ange, who found a credit card she lost in Mallorca after retracing a forty-seven-mile bike ride, went through my entire closet and came up empty-handed.

"Okay," Molly said, once we got down to my closet. "Where did you put it, and where has Ange looked?"

"I put it in this drawer in a manila envelope, because it needs to be in a dark place, and Ange looked through all the drawers and all the clothes, and she couldn't find it."

Molly scanned my closet and the built-in set of six drawers.

"It's behind the drawers," she declared and then pulled out the drawer I had put the manila envelope in, turned her phone light on, and shined it to the back of the drawer, and there it was. My manila envelope.

"This is definitely my mom fucking with me. Throwing all these kids at me, forcing me to love them, without the help of LSD," I told her.

I had spoken to a numerologist at the beginning of winter because I love all that stuff, and he told me that my mother had all my dogs and then he named each of them: Chunk, Tammy, Bert, and Bernice. I didn't bother telling the numerologist that Bernice was still with me, because I understood she was on her way out. I always thought my mother had something to do with my dogs, because my dogs always did stuff to remind me of her, like inhale brie cheese, leave the room when people came over, or look at me the way she did whenever I did something outrageous—like, *Really?*

The numerologist told me that there were many children around me on earth and that my mother is laughing her ass off in the spirit world and wants me to know that she loves seeing me with all the kids—and that even though I complain, she knows I secretly love it.

"Yes, this all tracks," I said.

The more dog training classes I did, the more I recognized the parallels between training a dog and parenting all kids.

Time spent is what they all need. The more time I spent with Doug, the more he calmed down. The more time I spent with all these kids, the more secure they seemed to feel. I had proved to this community in Whistler that I was reliable, dependable, on time, and that I was going to keep showing up. Now I had to do that for Doug. A much less stimulating endeavor when someone doesn't listen to any commands.

By week two of his dog training, Doug was suspended from his doggy group for being too aggressive. A parent's worst nightmare. It had been only two weeks ago that he had been called compassionate. The trainer explained that in large packs of dogs there is a hierarchy that is built, and Doug was clearly trying to stake his claim as a top alpha.

I applied what I had learned with the girls and started taking him out on hikes and walks by myself, and he quickly made friends with my neighbor's dog, Sequoia. The two of them would roll around in the snow, bite each other's ears, and drag each other down snowbanks. It seemed borderline violent, but my trainer told me that this was what dogs do, and that Doug being his age now of eleven months meant that he was comparable to a teenage boy and he needed to get his energy out. Masturbating into socks would be next.

Most mornings, my neighbor and I would alternate taking Sequoia and Doug to play with each other so that they could burn off some of their energy. On any given day, you could find me in my waterproof ski pants and jacket, Sorel boots, with four doggy leashes wrapped around my waist, and a fanny pack filled with dog treats, yelling, "Come, sit, stay, and good boy." I don't believe all dog trainers are lesbians, but they sure look like lesbians, and that's what I definitely looked like every day. Someone who was transitioning into a lesbian, who was also a fucking camp counselor.

All of my friends fell so in love with Doug and Bernice that I accrued a long waiting list of people who wanted to watch them. The bigger kids and adults wanted Doug, and his dance card filled up rather quickly. I would split Doug and Bernice up a lot, in an attempt to give Bernice a reprieve from her new big brother, who had the energy of someone on crystal meth.

I love asking parents who their favorite children are because the answers are pretty consistent among men and women. Women are loath to admit they have a favorite child, while men are readily able to admit who they prefer, or at the very least, they admit to having a favorite. One of the best answers I ever heard to this question came from one of my doctors who said, "Whichever child needs me the most at that time."

I loved that answer for three reasons: because it's honest; and because men love to be needed. The third reason is that it sums up exactly how I feel about all kids, whether they are my nieces, nephews, Oopsie, Whoopsie, Poopsie, or any of the other kids I spend my time hanging out with. Whichever one needs me the most is who's getting me.

As the winter came to an end, it became clear to me that Whoopsie needed me the most. I had noticed that when she and Oopsie visited, she seemed moody, always on the verge of a fight with her sister. I knew she needed a strong female role model who was not her mother, and she needed to be made to feel like a priority. I wanted to do that for her, to make sure she felt loved.

So I invited her and another friend's daughter from Whistler to go with me to Washington, D.C., where I was one of the comedians honoring Kevin Hart as he received the Mark Twain Prize. I knew this would be a night for them to remember. The girls would be surrounded by all these huge stars and they'd get to take pictures with so many famous people that night. I wanted to show them about professionalism (mine), and I wanted to show them that the sky was the limit. The girls had so much fun hanging out with Kevin Hart, while I yelled at him repeatedly at the after-party for being bad in bed. I have never had sex with Kevin Hart, but it just seems like someone who works so much wouldn't be good in bed.

I spent the evening trying to get Kevin to make a video for my twelve-year-old buddy Calvin, who is a huge Kevin Hart fan. Kevin was too drunk to focus at the after-party—after all, he had just been showered with fifteen tributes from all of his famous friends and was getting a huge award—so the next morning when he FaceTimed me to blame me for getting him so drunk, and to tell me that I'm a terrible influence, I said he needed to make Calvin his video before we ever spoke again. I posted the video on my Instagram as a split screen along with the video of Calvin watching the message from Kevin, and it was about as cute as it gets.

The next day, I scheduled a tour at George Washington University to plant some seeds in Whoopsie's head about her future. We looked at dorm rooms, at their massive gym and other facilities, and we talked with the dean of admissions about what would be required for her to be accepted there. Whoopsie had turned the beat around, was getting A's in English and history and couldn't get enough praise from me for doing so. She would send me screen grabs of all her grades after each test. I learned from the parenting coach that it was important not only to relay how proud I was of her but to impress upon her how proud she should be of herself. That hard work yields results.

After our tour of GW, I took the girls on a tour of D.C. This is the other thing children make you do. Get up, and plan activities. I took them to see the White House, the Treasury Building, and the Daughters of the American Revolution Museum. We sat outside the Smithsonian, and they drilled me with questions about history, the government, slavery, and what happens inside the Treasury Department. Whoopsie was engaged and curious, and for the first time I saw a young woman in her. I could envision her out in the world, making a life for herself, becoming successful, leaving high school behind in the dust. We went to a food truck and ordered some lunch, and sat on a park bench while both girls drilled me with more questions.

"So, you basically just make a living being yourself?" my friend's daughter asked.

"Yes, I suppose that's true," I said, realizing in that moment I had accomplished exactly what I set out to do when I drove across country at nineteen.

I went on to tell them about my childhood and adolescent angst. I shared a few stories about how terrible I had been as a teenager and said that at some point I was able to get focused and turn it all around. Even as a young person, what I longed for the most was financial security. I wanted to provide that for my family and anyone else I could help, because my parents were a financial hurricane. I wanted my brothers and sisters and nieces and nephews to feel the financial security that we had lacked growing up. I envisioned myself becoming the matriarch of our family. This is the role I had daydreamed about, and it had all come true.

I shared that I always wanted some distant aunt or uncle to notice my potential and become the apple of their eye, so that's what I've tried to do with my nieces and nephews, and what I wanted to do with Oopsie and Whoopsie. To instill in all of them that they are never alone and that nothing can ever get too bad because I'll always be in their corner. But, even more than that, to help them build the same self-security and stability. To be able to lean on people when they need help and, in turn, help people when they need it.

I told them that any success of mine was not my own. That it also belongs to all the people who helped me achieve it and to all the people who continue to make my success possible. For me, it is about sharing myself with the public, understanding that it's my fans who have allowed me to make a living off being myself. So it's my responsibility not only to share who I am with them but also to share my light with other people who need a boost. I think of my success as a giant circle of light around me, and opening myself up and allowing my light to shine on others only makes my light bigger and more ebullient. To never hoard success or claim it as your own. It belongs to more than just you. And to know that the most important metric of success is how willing you are to share it with others, and how diligent you are about storing up a surplus of kindness for strangers.

I wanted to plant seeds of hope in their brains. To show them that dreams are where the magic lies.

.   .   .

That was my last winter with Bernice. I lost her shortly after I returned to Los Angeles.

Bernice felt so loved that winter. Calvin and all the other little kids loved on her and spoiled her. Every night, she came into my room and put her paws on the edge of my bed so that I would pick her up. It was all I ever wanted: for her to know that I was going to be there to love her and protect her and be a real mother to my baby bear. And at the end, I rubbed her in her special spot behind her right ear while she drifted off from her mother's arms to my mother's arms.

When I got back from saying goodbye to Bernice, I sat on my bed and thought about all the love that came Bernice's way. Doug hopped up on the bed and came and put his head on my lap. He jumps on the bed all the time, but he doesn't stay for longer than a cuddle. This time, he lay next to me all night, sensing my heart was broken for my baby Bernice. None of my dogs—from Chunk to Tammy to Bert and Bernice—have ever comforted me in distress. Chunk would leave the room when I cried, because I believe he couldn't bear to see me sad. Bert and Bernice didn't care if I was sad, and Tammy was out to fucking lunch. She wanted to be with me all the time, but it was me comforting her, not the other way around. Doug was, in fact, compassionate, just as the dog walker had told me after his very first walk.

Oh, how my life had changed. Fatherhood, a winter filled with children, one of them about to go to college, another dog gone, and a new dog who was everything I could have hoped for. Snuggly, full-bodied, compassionate, black. Another era over, and another era beginning. Grateful for every single laugh and every single tear. Grateful to all the children who helped love up my baby bear on her last winter, and grateful to all of the children who taught me how to love.

But I'm good with children for a minute. It's enough.

Full Circle

J ane Fonda reached out to me when I was in Whistler and asked if I could come back to Los Angeles for a climate change event she was hosting against Big Oil. Of course, I said yes. It would require me to leave Whistler earlier than I had planned, but this was a request from Jane, so I packed up, left Whistler for the season, and headed home.

The next week I received an email from Jane:

Chelsea,

It meant a lot to me that you promised and you followed through, leaving your beloved slopes to attend the Gagosian event. That wasn't an easy thing for you to do, but you stuck to your word and not only showed up, you were in a good mood, spoke to the press, and did your job. Have you any idea how rare that is? I wanted to have famous people there to not only bring out the press, but to show the oil companies that we have heft on our side and they'd better think twice. For 2 months, I was on the phone and emailing. You are a rare one, Chelsea. It means a lot. And thanks for the nice things you said about me. More paintings are being sold every day and Wendy Schmidt pledged another $5 million‼ what a mensch. Whew.

Thanks, Chelsea
Love You, Jane

I had seen Jane Fonda many times since the night she had called me out on my bad behavior. She invited me to her eightieth birthday, and I made sure not to blow it. I went, I even danced, I hung out, spoke to everyone, and left before I could do any serious damage. It was my first attempt to prove to her that I would only be on my best behavior from here on out. And I kept trying to prove it to her. I showed up when she had hip surgery. A few friends and I went to her house to hang with her. We've done fundraisers together, and then I had her on my podcast. I redeemed myself with Jane and there was such value in that—in proving to someone that you are indeed the person they thought you could be.

Growth spurts aren't always linear. They happen in cycles, and they don't always show up right after the pain. We get hurt, injured, or experience great loss and pain, and often we want to fast-forward to be fully healed. Or, sometimes, we find ourselves stuck in our own pain because of a terrible loss that immobilizes us. Depending on the injury, healing can take days, or years. We always have a part in our own healing. And we always have the ability to wake up and try again.

To remind ourselves that life is filled with second and third chances, and it is up to us to jump when given the opportunity to try again. To never focus on past mistakes for too long, and instead to focus on showing up as the newer, improved version of yourself, and trusting that people will take notice. To never give up at getting better, and if it's not working for you one day, tuck yourself into bed, and try again the next day, and then keep trying. You're a woman, after all. You are one of the most powerful creatures on the planet. You'll get where you're going.

Woman

When I look back at all the things you've been through—from your hard lemonade stand, to driving across country alone at nineteen, to sitting across the table from Woody Allen—I am reminded that you are a force.

You are a rebel, a loudmouth, someone who was never going to settle for the status quo. Someone who knows there is always more, and that you can keep getting better, and that what you've always been searching for was a limitless freedom TO BE.

You have lost your way many times, but with fierce determination you have always found your way back to yourself. You are passionate and indefatigable in your desire to grow, learn, and care for others. You have stood up when others have sat down or looked away. You have picked people up off the floor and stood by them when no one else wanted to. You have sat with people and their grief for days, months, years. You go to people when they are at their lowest, and you give them hope.

The biggest gift you have given to others is to be there, to listen, and to hold people in their darkest moments. Remember when you sat beside your friend for a year when she needed you the most? You did that, and then you walked away when it was over. You have shown up; you have made an impact in people's lives.

You didn't know that was who you were going to be, but you became that for many people—many of whom you will never even meet. You are a healer. You wanted fame and fortune, and you got that, but all of that was an avenue to help heal. You heal people, and you healed yourself. You are valuable, and you are dependable. You're always on time. You never leave people waiting, and you are generous—not only with your time, but with your love. You are kind. You care so much about people; about women, about children, about doing the right thing.

You are going to keep loving out, to be more loved, and to sparkle when the sun is not shining. You have seen and done so much, and you're not even fifty! That's right, sister. You're only a year away from turning fifty years old! Can you believe you're still *alive* at fifty? It's not as old as it used to be. You look better than ever, and you finally have the body you've always wanted. You're beautiful. And you can ski like a fucking champ. You even have that ski house you always wanted.

You never went to college, but you've sent about fifty other people to college. How cool is that? You have one dog. Sometimes, you have two. You don't speak any languages other than limited Spanish, even though you've been taking Spanish class for years. You'll get it, one day. I now know you. You'll get it done. You have friends around the world who would show up for you at the drop of a hat, and YOU HAVE LIVED. You are vibrant, you are alive, and you are LIVING. YOUR LIFE HAS BEEN A DREAM.

You are a learner and a reader. You are so smart, even I am sometimes shocked by all that you know. Remember all the times you thought you were stupid? You have written six *New York Times* bestsellers. What stupid person does that?

Your family is a gift, and you are a gift to each of them. You show up. Forget about the mistakes, of which there were many. You aren't your mistakes. You're not going to repeat those mistakes anymore—

and if you slip up, you will make it right. You are a full circle. I'm so proud of you.

You have been loved fiercely, you have broken hearts, and you have been broken yourself. Your heart has broken, your body has broken down, and your mind has, at times, led you astray. Those were all signals to slow down and reassess. Today you are a success. You stood on the shoulders of giants and helped break open even more doors for women. You have misbehaved, and then corrected, and then misbehaved again, and then corrected some more.

Now it's your job to keep that candle lit, and not to let anyone, including yourself, blow it out. You are effulgent. You are true. You are a bright beam of generosity. Don't stop what you're doing, because you are on your way to great things. Hold on to the light. Look in the mirror every day and tell yourself, Hello, beautiful, what great things are we going to get up to today?

Acknowledgments

My editor, Whit Frick; my agents Christy Fletcher and Georgia Bodnar; the entire Dial Press and Random House team; my publicity team, Align, for being the absolute best team and for loving me so hard. I love you back twice as hard, Nicole, Paul, Alec, Taylor, Sophie, and Caroline. Nicole Perez, Sharon Jackson, and Whit for reading and rereading and rereading. I also want to thank the people who run my life: Molly, Karen, Mabel, Felix, Tanner, and Carlos, oh, and Darling. I always want to thank Darling. These are my everyday people who always have my best interest and always look out for me. And to my family, for providing me with endless material.

About the Author

Chelsea Handler is a writer, comedian, producer, TV host, activist, and the author of six consecutive *New York Times* bestsellers. She hosted the late-night talk show *Chelsea Lately* on the E! network from 2007 to 2014 and released a documentary series, *Chelsea Does,* on Netflix in January 2016. In 2016 and 2017, Handler hosted the talk show *Chelsea* on Netflix. Her Netflix comedy special, *Revolution,* was released in 2022 and is now streaming.